"The joy of the series . . . lies in encountering the various turns through which each of their authors has been put by his or her object. The object predominates, sits squarely center stage, directs the action. The object decides the genre, the chronology, and the limits of the study. Accordingly, the author has to take her cue from the *thing* she chose or that chose her. The result is a wonderfully uneven series of books, each one a *thing* unto itself."

Julian Yates, *Los Angeles Review of Books*

". . . edifying and entertaining . . . perfect for slipping in a pocket and pulling out when life is on hold."

Sarah Murdoch, *Toronto Star*

". . . a sensibility somewhere between Roland Barthes and Wes Anderson."

Simon Reynolds, author of *Retromania: Pop Culture's Addiction to Its Own Past*

OBJECT LESSONS

A book series about the hidden lives of ordinary things.

Series Editors:

Ian Bogost and Christopher Schaberg

Advisory Board:

Sara Ahmed, Jane Bennett, Jeffrey Jerome Cohen,
Johanna Drucker, Raiford Guins, Graham Harman,
renée hoogland, Pam Houston, Eileen Joy, Douglas
Kahn, Daniel Miller, Esther Milne, Timothy Morton,
Kathleen Stewart, Nigel Thrift, Rob Walker, Michele White.

In association with

LOYOLA
UNIVERSITY
NEW ORLEANS

Georgia | Center for
Tech | Media Studies

BOOKS IN THE SERIES

luggage

SUSAN HARLAN

BLOOMSBURY ACADEMIC
NEW YORK · LONDON · OXFORD · NEW DELHI · SYDNEY

BLOOMSBURY ACADEMIC
Bloomsbury Publishing Inc
1385 Broadway, New York, NY 10018, USA

BLOOMSBURY, BLOOMSBURY ACADEMIC and the Diana logo
are trademarks of Bloomsbury Publishing Plc

First published in the United States of America 2018

Cover design: Alice Marwick

A catalog record for this book is available from the Library of Congress.

ISBN: PB: 978-1-5013-2929-6
ePDF: 978-1-5013-2931-9
eBook: 978-1-5013-2930-2

Series: Object Lessons

Typeset by Deanta Global Publishing Services, Chennai, India
Printed and bound in the United States of America

To find out more about our authors and books visit www.bloomsbury.com
and sign up for our newsletters.

For Beryl, my beat-up old red
bumper-stickered car, now deceased,
who made all my road trips possible

CONTENTS

INTRODUCTION: TRAVEL AND ITS OBJECTS

There is something about baggage claim. Waiting for your suitcase. I have always liked it, perhaps because it is such a boring activity, but one with such purpose. And I like it because it is about being with strangers, if only for a time— all those faces from the flight that you will never see again. Sometimes I pick out the correct baggage carousel not by looking at the screen that tells you where to go, but by looking around for my fellow passengers. Where have they congregated? Ah. There they are. And everyone stands there, waiting for the carousel to start up and for the bags to come out, not sure what to do with themselves. Or they get on their phones and start talking and texting. Maybe they're thinking about the flight, thinking that they're glad that it's over. Glad to be home or wherever they are. Maybe they're wishing that they hadn't checked their bags. Maybe they weren't planning to, but the flight attendant took their suitcases away at the last minute—because of a lack of storage space or because they were too large. And when your suitcase is taken from you, you know that baggage claim awaits.

There is a tenuous and temporary sense of community around the baggage carousel. We might help one another to haul our bags off the carousel or load them back on when we determine that we have claimed the wrong black suitcase. It's not that we really care about one another, but we feel somehow stuck in the situation. This bond, if it is a bond, doesn't usually exist on the plane, where cramped spaces conspire to create an environment defined by controlled tensions. Then, at our destination, we're set free, only to find that ten minutes later, a number of us are brought back together again, in another place, before we can move to the next phase of our trips and lives. On the plane, I try to maintain a psychological distance from my seatmates so as not to get trapped in small talk or, worse, actual talk that turns out to be terrible. But when I see my fellow passengers again in baggage claim, I feel almost as if I know them, as if we have been though something together, and I almost wish I could talk to them. And we have been through something: an utterly banal experience that means nothing in particular and will be forgotten almost immediately, perhaps as soon as we walk through the sliding glass doors, out into the heat or the cold.

I watch suitcase after suitcase on the groaning carousel, thinking about which bags might belong to which people, these people that I don't know and will never know. Some of the bags are heavy and unwieldy and marked with OVERWEIGHT tags. Some are shrink-wrapped in clear plastic, like enormous leftovers in the fridge. I suppose this is supposed to serve as protection against theft, but it must be a hassle for the TSA to remove, if they need to. I think about which suitcases I like more than my own, and I notice which ones are particularly ugly. If someone is traveling with matched luggage, you can identify their bags once they claim the first one. I look at the oddly shaped cardboard boxes and wonder what they contain. There is always a variety of luggage in baggage claim. Most of the bags in the plane's overhead compartments are the same: black rolling carry-ons, or Roll aboards. Some people tie scarves or bandanas around these suitcases to set them apart. Like a uniform, a black Roll aboard reveals nothing about its owner. It is unreadable, opaque. But sew a patch onto it or affix a bright baggage tag in the shape of a football or a turtle, and suddenly it becomes something else. In baggage claim, you see bags in all shapes, sizes, and colors. And the boring black suitcases cause confusion. *Excuse me, but I think that one is mine. No, I'm pretty sure this one is mine—let me check the tag. Oh, I'm so sorry—it looks just like mine.* This is the baggage carousel dance. Trying to reclaim our property. Trying to identify it. Some people monogram their luggage. This is practical—a monogram helps you to pick out you suitcase—but it is also tied to identity in deeper ways. A monogram is the textual distillation of your identity and a declaration of ownership. *This is mine.* It becomes another brand: your brand alongside the brand of the suitcase; a mark the self, endlessly reproducible and immediately recognizable.

Some people plaster their suitcases with stickers from places they have been, although this is a bit old-fashioned now. The stickers create a partial narrative of the bag's owner. In *Black Lamb and Gray Falcon*, Rebecca West notes of one passenger, on a train from Salzburg to the former Yugoslavia, that "the labels on his suitcase suggested he was either an actor or dancer, and indeed his slender body was as unnaturally compressed by exercise as by a corset."[1] The suitcase's labels allow her to guess the profession of its owner, and his body supports what his luggage suggests. The design of suitcase labels in the nineteenth and twentieth centuries often originated from travel posters, but they were not intended to generate a desire to travel, as was the case with the posters; they operated as mementos that proved one's status as well-traveled and cultured.[2] In a current iteration, luggage labels mark not only cultural capital but also actual capital: Louis Vuitton offers a "personalization service" whereby they will customize a new bag with patches of "exotic locales" and vintage LV logos.[3] The resulting bag represents an ersatz and nostalgic engagement with the history of luggage labels. You don't need to have been anywhere; a luggage brand will create this narrative for you. But in their true form, luggage labels narrated where you had been and what you had seen. They were proof of personal experience. And, as souvenirs that quite literally affixed themselves to your suitcase, they were indelible. They might become worn down over time, or you might pick at the edges of one in a moment of boredom, but once you stuck them to your suitcase, they were there to stay, unlike memories. Luggage labels mark the unrecoverability of a trip once it is concluded.

All of travel is, to some extent, liminal: it is about being neither here nor there, always in the process of going and coming and becoming. On a train late at night, you might feel this in the jerking of your train car on the tracks or in the inky invisibility of the landscape outside your window, the void through which you move. You might feel it on a long drive, after a number of hours, when you begin to map out time in the songs you have played or your level of hunger or your need to pee. But perhaps because baggage claim stops the forward movement of a journey and asks you to wait, it becomes a threshold space with its own sense of time. It's not that time stops or is held in suspension, although it may feel that way, particularly if you are tired, and baggage claim tends to be a place of tired people. It's that another space is carved out of the in-between time of travel, and this time is temporary even when it feels interminable—even when your bag is the last one to come off the carousel or when it doesn't come at all, and you have to visit the dreaded lost luggage office. Even in those situations, you know that you will eventually leave the airport because airports are all about leaving. Sometimes I watch the last unclaimed bag on another carousel, wondering where its owner is (maybe just in the bathroom?). Like a carousel at a fair, a baggage carousel is a closed loop: it goes around and around and, ultimately, it goes nowhere. Baggage claim brings you close to a feeling of nothingness. When your mind is almost cleared out, when you're not quite home and not quite not-home, when you're in this nothing place, you wonder if you might also be nothing, but you're too tired to worry about it much. So you pick out a bag on the carousel and watch until it disappears into a hole in the wall.

This book is about what we bring with us when we travel. It is about bags and what they contain. The history of luggage *is* the history of travel: how we have traveled, and why, and where, and what we have packed. It is virtually impossible to think of traveling without luggage. (There are certain erotic implications to checking into a hotel with someone and without luggage.) The presence of a suitcase means that you are going somewhere or that you have come from somewhere. Paul Fussell notes that "the traveler's world is not the ordinary one, for travel itself, even the most commonplace, is an implicit quest for anomaly."[4] Sometimes we are just going on a business trip or going to visit a relative, but traveling takes us into another space apart from the everyday, both literally and figuratively. Heroes know this. A quest is certainly one way to travel—or one way to think about travel, as it is for Fussell. And heroes need to bring things with them. Odysseus's ships are well stocked with food (including goats) and drink, which—along with the spoils of hunting and the luxuries of his hostesses—allow him to survive in the liminal space between war and home, a space in which he chose to remain for some time.[5] Poets from Alfred, Lord Tennyson to

C. P. Cavafy have understood that Odysseus desires his home, but he is also alienated from it. Even fears it. His supplies—part of a larger category of luggage we might refer to as gear, stores, or cargo—create a sense of home abroad, both reminding him of the domestic sphere that awaits him and allowing him to continue to dwell in a space of deferment. In the medieval romance *Sir Gawain and the Green Knight*, Sir Gawain isn't very well provided for on his quest. He leaves the comforts of the court behind and sets off into a hostile world, to prove himself and answer the Green Knight's challenge. He is cold and miserable. He is uncomfortable. He is alone. Joseph Campbell knew that for the hero to ultimately be reintegrated into society, he has to separate himself from it to seek adventure, endure tests and challenges, and prove himself.[6] This is the world, and the system of values, that Cervantes spoofs in *Don Quixote.* The "paragon and model of all knights errant" Don Quixote travels with only his sad nag Rocinante and some rusted and mildewed armor he does his best to clean.[7] When he stops at the inn that he takes for a "castle-fortress," the innkeeper finds his bridle, lance, shield, and corselet absurd.[8] This is the luggage of the real, legitimate knight, the accouterments of a lost figure that Don Quixote reads about in his books and seeks to emulate, a figure utterly out of place in his world. But as he is not a real knight, so his luggage is not real knightly luggage. Don Quixote loves fantasy, and he understands how tempting it is to turn fantasy into your own reality. This is his baggage: that he wishes to belong to a world that has passed away.

People have always moved from one place to another, and they have needed to bring things with them. Herodotus was a traveler, although the extent of his travels remains unknown. *The Histories* (from the fifth century BCE) is the work of someone who was interested not only in wars, but also in differences between cultures.[9] Romans under Augustus traveled for their health, to visit oracles, and to attend sporting events.[10] Most people walked, but some rode on horseback or in wagons, although roads were narrow and hazardous.[11] But if you were mobile, this was probably because you needed to be—or you had a duty to perform. Maybe you were a merchant. Maybe you were a soldier. Your reason for traveling and your mode of transportation determined what you brought with you. The materials of travel have developed to respond to travelers' needs, desires, and tastes. In medieval Europe, aristocratic European families traveled with chests, sometimes adorned with heraldic devices. These coffers were often made of leather, wood, and iron and were designed to protect your belongings from the elements and from theft. They were both portable and domestic property: after all, a trunk or chest is also a piece of furniture. But not everyone traveled with trunks. If you were setting off on a pilgrimage, you needed to travel light. In the high Middle Ages, pilgrims traveled to sites such as Rome, Canterbury Cathedral in England, Santiago de Compostela in northwest Spain, and of course the Holy Land. Pilgrims like Saint James are frequently depicted as carrying a small purse, along with a staff, a broad-brimmed hat, and a shell-shaped badge. Missal boxes, flasks, and pouches could be hung from the staff or from loops on one's belt.[12] Santo Brasca of Milan advised that pilgrims bring gold and silver, food (including sausages, sugar, preserved sweetmeats, and fruit syrup), and two extra bags, each filled with one hundred Venetian ducats: one bag to cover the expenses of the voyage and the other one for illness "or other circumstances."[13] Some pilgrims wore small containers to carry sacred materials: these containers were luggage, jewelry, and souvenirs all at once. It was customary for pilgrims to bring offerings to the shrines they visited, including liturgical vessels and elaborate priestly vestments. In Chaucer's *The Canterbury Tales*, the Pardoner has his own fake religious baggage: he sells holy relics that are actually pigs' bones.

But pilgrimages were undertaken for religious purposes, not for leisure.[14] A pilgrimage is travel as "a penance and a purge."[15] When we talk about traveling today, we tend to associate it with leisure. Vacations. Tourism is about the pursuit of pleasure and entertainment, as well as consumption—both of things and places. Prior to the mid-nineteenth century, a "vacation" referred not to a time set aside for recreation and travel, but to students' and teachers' breaks from school or college.[16] Today, tourism is the world's largest service sector industry, and although this industry often draws on the traditions of the quest and the medieval pilgrimage in its understanding of "journeys," its origins lie in the European Grand Tour.[17] From the seventeenth century, these lengthy journeys were undertaken by (primarily

English) aristocrats as a form of education and a means of gaining experience, as Sir Francis Bacon outlined in his essay "On Travel," which was published in 1625. The Grand Tour was required of any self-respecting English gentleman—or aspiring gentleman—for 200 years.[18] It gives way to citizens' travel in the nineteenth century.[19] Those who undertook the Grand Tour sought knowledge and pleasure. They were tourists of sorts, although the term "tourist" doesn't appear until 1800, and they carried a lot of luggage: trunks that often contained elaborate cabinets and drawers, not unlike bringing a closet or wardrobe along.[20] Sometimes these men traveled by ship. They also traveled by coach, "a non- or anti-plebeian vehicle, heavy, tall, exclusive, private, and expensive" that was sometimes equipped with false floors and other hiding places for valuables.[21] These coaches were, in a sense, also luggage. Gentlemen on the Grand Tour often traveled with servants, so they were not obligated to manage their trunks themselves.

Sometimes it is difficult to distinguish between a traveler and his or her luggage. We become our things. An anonymous seventeenth-century French etching *Habit de Mallettier Coffrettier (Costume of a luggage-maker)* depicts a man with a trunk under each arm, a number of pouches hanging off his belt, pouches slung over his shoulder, and a trunk balanced on his head (and fashioned into a hat). This master of design has transformed *himself* into luggage: the embodiment of efficiency and luxury. He is not in a carriage. He is not on horseback. He travels on foot, carrying all of

FIGURE 1

this with him. He is his own creation. Even his torso looks like a trunk.

In Jacques Joseph Tissot's painting *Waiting for the Train (Willesden Junction)* (c.1871–73), a woman stands on a north London train platform, surrounded by her trunks and bags. Here, too, her possessions take over: she is less the subject of the painting than what she carries with her. She holds a bouquet of flowers, an umbrella, and a scarf in her arms,

FIGURE 2

reminders that bourgeois travel is largely defined by the *stuff* you bring with you. But her full arms are also reminders that she will not handle her bags: a not-yet-visible porter will transport them onto the train when it arrives. This painting depicts a very different kind of travel from the Grand Tour: a woman traveling in a new way, by train. And she is waiting, a crucial part of train travel. She is subject to a schedule.

Although European travel was restricted or impossible during the Napoleonic Wars, the years after the war brought major advances in the technologies of travel, most notably the steam engine. Travel by rail dates to the early 1800s, and by the 1860s and 1880s, sleeping and dining cars added to the comfort of the experience.[22] Railroads made mass tourism possible. And while trunks remained a popular form of luggage, luggage designs increasingly answered to the needs of travelers who were setting off to inns and hotels.[23] You might purchase an eating kit with cutlery, a cup, a spice container, and a corkscrew, cases for men's and women's toilet articles (made of glass, silver, tortoiseshell and ivory), stiff, patterned cardboard bandboxes to carry personal effects, and leather portmanteaus designed in a cylindrical shape with a top compartment accessible by a fitted flap.[24] Although some portmanteaus, were quite simple (and were intended to be strapped to the back of a saddle), their designs became more elaborate, and they began to resemble modern suitcases. Eating kits were handy, as your inn might not provide these things. You might also wish to bring pens, paper, a lantern, a teapot, and candles with you.[25] As the English flocked to the seaside, they had to make sure that their luggage contained a bathing suit and a beach bag.

But tourism was only one form of travel in the nineteenth century. Travel was not always about pleasure, nor was it always about middle-class comforts. Sometimes it was about getting from one place to another, which could be uncomfortable and dangerous. This was the age of the steamship and the sailing ship. Today, one in seven Americans has been on a cruise.[26] And while the cruise industry would like customers to believe that the cruise is the direct descendant of steamships and ocean liners, this is not the case. The steamships of the early nineteenth century "were based on the economics of the great immigrant trade that had defined passenger shipping during the early part of the century . . . a rigid stratification between an opulent first-class world above decks and the cramped spaces below."[27] These passengers were referred to as "talking cargo," and those who traveled in steerage found themselves in a space not unlike a cargo hold.[28] Sailing ships of the period were nicknamed "coffin ships," with death rates above 10 percent of their steerage passengers.[29] In the later part of the century, steamship technology improved conditions a little and cut travel time, but travel was still hardly luxurious. With the First World War came ventilation, toilets, and running water for steerage-class passengers, but also the end of the United States' period of mass migration.[30]

By the 1860s, the *Great Eastern* was crossing the Atlantic in twelve days, with its 3,000 passengers enjoying all manner of luxuries, from hot baths to fine food and champagne.[31] And for wealthy travelers, luggage not only protected your possessions; it also proclaimed your class position. How much you brought with you on a trans-Atlantic crossing depended on how much money you had. Until the 1930s, dinner dress on the best ocean liners was white tie, which was only one of the outfits you needed for an average day and evening. It was standard for a first-class passenger to bring twenty pieces of luggage containing four changes of clothing per day.[32] But only some of this luggage was kept in your cabin, including a steamer trunk, which resembled a portable closet with hangers and drawers. And then there were Louis Vuitton's trunks. Founded in 1854 at 4 Rue Neuve-des-Capucines in Paris, Louis Vuitton became famous for his trunks in wood, canvas, brass, and iron, which could be customized; you might order one to hold 30 pairs of shoes. The company even made luggage that attached to the sides of hot-air balloons. (In 2007, Louis Vuitton designed custom luggage for Wes Anderson's film *The Darjeeling Limited*.) And wealthy travelers didn't need to exercise packing restraint as they did not handle their luggage themselves: porters moved it on and off ships and trains. Porters could be hired in London's train stations until the beginning of the twentieth century.[33] In the United States, the former slaves hired by George Pullman to work in sleeping cars were known as Pullman porters. Under the Jim Crow laws, they moved white passengers' bags in and out of train cars in which they were not allowed to travel. In 1925, they formed first all-black union—the Brotherhood of the Sleeping Car Porters—and were central to the advancement of the civil rights movement and the establishment of a black American middle class.[34]

The years surrounding the First World War were crucial for the development of American tourism. The outbreak of the war closed European resorts to American tourists and led to a boom in patriotism that was in line with the "See

America First" tourism slogan of the turn of the century. Railroads were expanding. Roads were improving. The first three decades of the twentieth century saw the popularizing of America's national parks.[35] Mass tourism continued to expand during the Depression, due largely to promotion and the rise of the two-week paid vacation for white-collar salaried workers from executives to clerical personnel in the early decades of the century.[36] Charles Lindbergh flight across the Atlantic in 1927 had glamorized international air travel in the American imagination, and he advised two major airlines: TWA and Pan American. TWA originally called itself "The Lindberg Line."[37] But by the mid-1930s, long-distance air travel was still rare in Europe and North America compared with travel by train or ship.[38]

By the 1920s, automobile travel was becoming popular, and the next few decades saw the rise of air travel. When we complain about the horrors of flying today and romanticize the past, we should remember that in 1939, it cost $750 to fly round-trip from New York City to France on Pan Am's *Dixie Clipper*, which is well over $11,000 today. In 1970, flying from New York to Hawaii would have cost you the equivalent of $2,700. But aircraft like the 707 and 747 made long-haul travel affordable.[39] As Elizabeth Becker notes, "By the 1960s the jet age of mass tourism was taking off. In 1958 a Pan American 707 flew from New York to Brussels, the first commercial jet flight across the Atlantic without stopping for refueling. . . . Lower fares and bargain flights followed. European countries relaxed passport restrictions and began to see tourism as an important economic engine."[40] Arthur Frommer's *Europe on $5 a Day* was published in 1960, offering middle-class Americans practical travel tips and reimagining the European vacation as something affordable. A GI who had been stationed in Berlin after the Second World War, Frommer packaged Europe not as an aristocratic Grand Tour of several months, but as a several-week tour that the middle classes could enjoy.[41] By the 1970s, industries in the "travel and tourism complex" were the largest advertisers in American newspapers.[42] The tourist was a sightseer, and sightseeing had its own luggage—camera bags, shoulder bags, and backpacks, which came into popular use after the Second World War—as well as "its own moral structure, a collective sense that certain sites must be seen."[43] When Delsey was founded in 1946, it manufactured leather cases for cameras. Sightseeing was both obligation and ritual, and the tourist had to prepare for these rites by packing the correct things. Frommer wasn't interested in providing information about sites you might see, as was the case with the *Baedeker* guides of the nineteenth century. Frommer told you how to navigate unfamiliar countries. He relieved you of the baggage, or anxiety, that only rich people could do this.

People traveling by rail, by car, and by plane needed suitcases. Suitcases of the nineteenth century were made of fiber or wicker, mock-leather, leather, or alligator or crocodile skin, in increasing order of grandness.[44] Linen, wool, and wicker were also popular materials. These cases—which were cases for suits—had wood or steel frames, and corners were often rounded out using brass or leather caps.[45] But materials changed in the twentieth century: nylon, aluminum, and polyester took over. American Tourister was founded in 1933 in Providence, Rhode Island, and by 1945, they were manufacturing lightweight "Hi-Taper" luggage for air travel. They designed the first molded luggage in the 1960s—hardside cases that could take the wear and tear of air travel—and tested their bags with flight attendants from major airlines. Founded in 1877 as a leather goods business in Milwaukee, Hartmann opened a manufacturing plant in Tennessee in 1956. And the Shwayder Trunk Manufacturing Company was founded in Denver in 1910. The owner Jesse Shwayder named one of his first designs after the biblical strongman Samson, and in 1966, the company became Samsonite. Compared to luggage today, these bags were still heavy, even when empty. They looked and felt like cases. It was not until 1972 that something close to the contemporary rolling suitcase came about. A man named Bernard Sadow affixed four casters and a short strap to a bag, and he held a patent for a short period of time.[46] This is the kind of suitcase that Joan Wilder (Kathleen Turner) drags behind her in *Romancing the Stone* (1984). Along with her high heels, the suitcase establishes her as ill-suited to the rugged jungle environment in which she finds herself, and ultimately Jack T. Colton (Michael Douglas) loses patience with her urban ways and throws it into a ravine. Although part of the joke is that women are bad packers and unable to survive without tons of stuff—an age-old misogynist cliché—this design is not in fact the most practical. Rolled in this way, a suitcase will wobble from side to side, always threatening to topple over, especially if you find yourself on a dirt road in the mountains of Colombia, trying to rescue your kidnapped sister. These suitcases are now a thing of the past. In 1987, Northwest Airlines pilot Robert Plath changed the orientation of the suitcase to upright and sideways and added an extendable handle. This was the birth of the now-ubiquitous Rollaboard suitcase, which was initially marketed only to flight crews. Once it became widely available, travelers no longer had to check their luggage, and within a year, the FAA had established guidelines for carry-on bags.[47]

Luggage is bound by rules. The first baggage rules were put in place in 1938. The Civil Aeronautics Board restricted bags to 40 pounds for domestic flights and 44 pounds for international travel. These restrictions were practical as space was limited, but as airplanes expanded, baggage allowances did too, and by the late 1970s, passengers could check two bags weighing up to 70 pounds each, free of charge. Peoplexpress was the first domestic line to charge for luggage, regardless of weight, but by 2010, virtually all domestic carriers charged for checked bags.[48] The practice is part of "unbundling," or charging à la carte (as with food), and it is a chief means by which airlines increase their revenue.[49] Commercial airlines now estimate 190 pounds per passenger, including his or her carry-ons, and 30 pounds per checked bag. Four hundred passengers and their luggage, or approximately 75,000 pounds, makes up only 10 percent of the total weight of a fully loaded 747. (Fuel often accounts for a third or more of a plane's total bulk.)[50] But you can still travel on Cunard's *Queen Mary* with unlimited luggage. Over time, luggage design and space have become standardized.[51] But there is still nothing standard about luggage: this is one of its object lessons.

This is the story of a suitcase and a trip.

I'm going to a conference in Atlanta, and I need to pack. Three days of seminars and panels and talks about Shakespeare. But a section of I-85 collapsed a few weeks ago, so I have decided to take another route. A scenic route. I feel like a drive. I get out my atlas and plot a trip from my home in central North Carolina to Helen, Georgia, a mock-Bavarian village one hour north of Atlanta. It's late morning, so if I pack the car and set off soon, I should be okay; I can stay in Helen tonight and head into the city tomorrow. And I can take my dog Millie with me and board her while I'm at the conference. This makes me happy as we always road-trip together.

I rummage around in my closet and select my orange hardside suitcase. It's not huge, but it's not carry-on size either, and there's no reason to pack efficiently when you're driving. You car can become your suitcase. Some things just stay in my car: instant coffee, a corkscrew, and a travel alarm clock in the glove compartment. Otherwise: sunblock, bug spray, umbrellas, tote bags, a picnic blanket, an atlas, and my CD binders from college that represent my music taste twenty years ago, but I find that with a few exceptions this is generally fine. It means that I listen to a lot of Indigo Girls when I drive. After twenty years, I can say with absolute certainty that I still don't understand "Galileo."

I don't have a packing technique. If I were flying and taking a small suitcase, I would fit things together more precisely, but as it is, I have more room than I need. I love the design of this suitcase because it opens to reveal two sides of equal size, like drawers, and each zips closed. This feels so contained and secure. I pack my conference clothes on one side (skirts, blouses, hose, a nice jacket, some jewelry, a small purse, a book bag) and my road trip clothes on the other. I pack a pair of heels that will match everything on the conference side. Some people pack their shoes in little pouches, but I just turn the soles to the outside of the suitcase. I have a road trip uniform that developed almost accidentally over the years: a long black cotton skirt (or two) that I can wear for a number of days in a row, white men's tank top undershirts (I buy another pack if I run out), and a big scarf/sarong to tie around my waist. And I bring a couple of other scarves to switch out. All of this goes on the road-tripping side of the suitcase. Also toiletries and some conference things: my laptop, my paper, and a few books—some work-related (Shakespeare) and some not (mostly poetry, not by Shakespeare). And my glasses. I put on my gold hoops from Target, a big gold and black enamel necklace that I bought at the gift shop of the New-York Historical Society years ago and wear almost every day, and my watch. All costume jewelry.

I load my suitcase into the car and throw in a flashlight and folding chair, which might come in handy. And I pack Millie's food, bed, and bowls. And bourbon. Two bottles of water. My sunglasses. She jumps in the back seat, where I fasten her into her dog seatbelt, and we leave around lunchtime, bound for the make-believe Alps, driving away from the real.

1 LUGGAGE AND SECRETS

Luggage holds secrets. Some of these secrets belong to the trunks and suitcases, and some of them do not. They might belong to history or to a person or to nothing at all. Some of these secrets are revealed, and some remain hidden, enclosed. And perhaps we want luggage to contain secrets because bags are so suggestive. In their emptiness or fullness, they suggest more than themselves. A suitcase that is closed—not even zipped closed, but simply closed—is like a bedside table or a medicine cabinet: it is off limits. Our luggage is private, but it goes with us in public. You do not rummage through someone else's bags—when it happens in Customs, it feels like a violation, as it does when your checked bag is searched. In this case, you find a piece of paper that tells you the invasion has taken place, and your possessions are put back in an imperfect manner that marks their disturbance.

In Tennessee Williams's *A Streetcar Named Desire*, Stanley rummages around in Blanche's trunk, throwing its contents all over the room. This violation prefigures his violation of her body—it is the first of two attacks—and by manhandling her personal possessions, he makes it clear that she will have no secrets in his house. Blanche's trunk is baggage, furniture, and character all at once, a heavy and unwieldy onstage presence that mirrors her own frail but nonetheless steely physicality. It contains, among other things, records of her lost ancestral home Belle Reve. It *is* Belle Reve on stage, in debased form, and to Stanley, the papers it contains promise an explanation of what happened to this ideal place. When he asks to see them (to prove that he has not been cheated out of his wife's supposed fortune), Blanche says, "Everything that I own is in that trunk," delineating not only the limits of the trunk, but also of her life. He starts to open its compartments, but she intercedes, producing a tin box filled with "thousands of papers stretching back over hundreds of years" that she hands over to him angrily: "Here all of them are, all papers! I hereby endow you with them! Take them, peruse them— commit them to memory, even! I think it's wonderfully fitting that Belle Reve should finally be a bunch of old papers in your big, capable hands!"[1] The house is no more than a pile of papers, and Blanche knows that the reader of these papers will not understand them.

For Blanche, her trunk is private. Its interiority is her interiority. In her work on ideas of homes in Georgian London, Amanda Vickery notes that understandings of privacy are linked not only to the domestic, but also to locked trunks, boxes, closets, and compartments. Although servants rarely had a bedroom, let alone a private bedroom, they had locked containers in which to store their possessions. Such locked boxes, trunks, and chests were a way to protect not only your things, but also your secrets. It was a space that was yours in a world in which so little was. You might also opt to keep any valuables on your person—in pockets, pouches, or lockets.[2] Some of these boxes were more portable than others. In the first print of William Hogarth's 1732 *Harlot's Progress*, Moll Hackabout arrives in London with a box the size of a large trunk. She dies in the end, and her trunk is ransacked.[3]

Spy thrillers and mysteries know that suitcases are emblems of secrecy, particularly if they are made of silver aluminum. In a John le Carré novel, a suitcase or briefcase might contain top-secret documents, unmarked bills, or stolen jewels. In all cases, the secrecy of the contents underscores their value. This idea is spoofed in *The Big Lebowski* (1998), when Walter (John Goodman) replaces the aluminum suitcase filled with money with his dirty laundry— what he calls "my dirty undies . . . laundry . . . the whites"— and throws it over the bridge. That this "ringer" is valueless suits a film in which the kidnapping that drives the (non-) plot has not even occurred. In *Dumb and Dumber* (1994), a suitcase that should be filled with money turns out to contain only IOU's, which Lloyd Christmas (Jim Carrey) deems "as good as money" as he is the one who has spent it all. Lloyd is also under the impression that the suitcase belongs to a man named "Samsonite" as he fails to understand the difference between a brand and a monogram.

Luggage often contains things that it should not. Luggage contains contraband. The artist Taryn Simon spent five days and nights (from November 16 to 20, 2009) at John F. Kennedy International Airport in New York City, photographing objects in both the US Customs and Border Protection Federal Inspection Site and the US Postal Service International Mail Facility, which Hans Ulrich Obrist refers to as "sites that are a contraband space, a space between America and other nations" in an introductory essay to the Gagosian exhibit catalogue.[4] The resulting project *Contraband* is, he notes, "an extended study of international transit, of the international currency of prohibited items, and especially of the tide of counterfeit goods that have flooded Western markets in the wake of relocation of production to the newly developing countries of the East."[5] Simon's 1,075 photographs of seized and detained items invoke Christian Boltanski's *Lost Property—Tramway* (1994), which gathered 5,000 forgotten objects.[6] Both Simon and Boltanski's work explore the histories and stories embodied in often banal or mundane things, things that are in many ways disposable before they are disposed of: knives, lighters, cigarettes. Simon documented luxury items, including gemstones, and valueless items, like apples. She documented counterfeit Louis Vuitton bags and other counterfeit items: erectile dysfunction medication, jeans, jewelry, Lacoste and Ralph Lauren shirts, and phones. Pirated movies, fitness DVDs, and educational DVDs. And memento mori objects that speak to an absent and violated animal world: animal corpses and skeletons, dead guinea pigs, deer blood, and antlers. And, finally, she photographed things identified simply as UNIDENTIFIED—embodiments of the unknown. Simon distinguished between objects that were smuggled and those that were mailed, suggesting that mailing "offers up a space of anonymity" and "anonymous desire" that smuggling does not.[7] To smuggle something, with your body or your luggage, is more personal, as your body becomes implicated in the concept, or space, of contraband. There are no people in these photographs: only things that suggest people. The photographs feel exhaustive while also underscoring the impossibility of exhaustiveness. Simon herself became sleep-deprived; she showered only once.[8] These trafficked items are caught in photographs, made still. But this stillness reminds you that they are defined by their motion, by their movement from one place to another, and by the interruption of this movement.

Sometimes luggage actually holds photographs. In 2007, three boxes of rolls of film containing 4,500 35-mm negatives of the Spanish Civil War taken by Robert Capa, Chim (David Seymour), and Gerda Taro arrived at the International Center for Photography in New York City. These materials were addressed to founder Cornell Capa, Robert's younger brother and the center's founder. The negatives had been lost since 1939, but had been found in Mexico City in the personal possessions of the Mexican ambassador to Vichy France. This discovery validated the rumor that such a suitcase existed but had been lost in the Second World War.[9] This bag held a history of violence: images that speak to, and of, the past. These photographs are not the only records of the war to be found in a suitcase. The 2015 film *Suite Française* was adapted from *Tempête en juin*, the first of two novels by the French author Irène Némirovsky that her daughters found in a suitcase and published in 2004. They had preserved the notebooks but had not examined them, having assumed that they were her diaries. The novel tells the story of the Nazi occupation of the town of Bussy following the bombings of Paris in June 1940 and the refugees from the city that sought shelter there. It is also about a love affair between a French woman and a German soldier. Némirovsky had planned to write a series of five novels, but she was Jewish, and in 1942 she was arrested and deported and died at Auschwitz. At the end of the film, the credits roll over shots of the manuscript itself, a reminder of how objects can be sheltered in a suitcase and protected in a way that subjects are not.

Sometimes suitcases hold more personal, private histories. In 2015, a trove of seventeenth-century dead letters was discovered in a leather trunk in the Netherlands. The trunk of 2,600 letters was presented to a postal museum in The Hague in 1926, but it was never studied. The letters are written in six languages and speak to the daily lives of peasants, merchants, and aristocrats. They had been placed in the trunk for safekeeping by Simon de Brienne and his wife Maria Germain, the postmaster and mistress in The Hague from 1676 to 1707, but their recipients never came to claim them.[10] An undelivered letter is "dead." Its life is linked to its recipient, by the act of being read. At the end of Herman Melville's *Bartleby the Scrivener*, we learn that the perplexing clerk Bartleby once worked in the Dead Letter Office. The narrator imagines the contents of these letters—perhaps a ring meant for a now-dead finger or a bank note or a pardon or good tidings—and these imagined things prompt his final exclamation, "Ah, Bartleby! Ah, humanity!"[11] In Melville's story, the dead letters are burned, but the found leather trunk kept these very things safe for hundreds of years. The trunk couldn't bring them back to life, but it could preserve them.

Letters tell personal histories. To read other people's mail, even if these people have been dead for centuries, is to enter into their stories and daily lives. But perhaps the longer a trunk or a suitcase endures, the more fascinating and illicit its secrets become. These are the kinds of secrets that Catherine Morland hopes to find in Jane Austen's satire of Gothic fiction *Northanger Abbey*. As a guest at the abbey, she comes across a "large high chest, standing back in a deep recess on one side of the fireplace" in her room.[12] The sight of this cedar chest and its tarnished silver lock engages her imagination and gives rise to a state of "motionless wonder": she observes that the handles are broken, "perhaps prematurely by some strange violence."[13] The "mysterious cipher" on the lid suggests that this is no ordinary trunk, and she suspects it may reveal dark secrets about the Tilneys, the family she is visiting. Fueled by her passion for novels such as Ann Radcliffe's *The Mysteries of Udolpho* and *The Romance of the Forest*, she seizes the lock with "trembling hands" and lifts it several inches, only to be interrupted by a maid and then by her friend Miss Tilney, who is less thrilled by the trunk than Catherine. She observes only that "I thought it might sometimes be of use holding hats and bonnets," were it not so difficult to open.[14] But Catherine is not to be discouraged. When she returns to her room after dinner (during a violent storm, of course), she notices an old-fashioned black cabinet and finds a promising roll of paper that is "pushed back into the further part of the cavity, apparently for concealment."[15] She is certain that this must contain the secrets she so desires: "She seized, with an unsteady hand, the precious manuscript, for half a glance sufficed to ascertain written characters."[16] Catherine reads the cipher on the trunk; Catherine reads this mysterious document. She is a reader, an interpreter, and she wants a text that is sufficiently thrilling. Indeed, her imagination transforms the room into a wildly Gothic scene:

> The very curtains of her bed seemed at one moment in motion, and at another the lock of her door was agitated, as if by the attempt of somebody to enter. Hollow murmurs seemed to creep along the gallery, and more than once her blood was chilled by the sound of distant moans.[17]

Catherine's environment may "seem" like the exciting and menacing world of the novels she devours, but it proves disappointingly quotidian. The next morning, when the sunlight allows her to peruse the roll of documents, she finds only an inventory of linen, a washing bill, and a farrier's bill.[18]

These texts tell a story of the daily workings of the abbey, nothing more, and Catherine feels the full force of "the absurdity of her recent fancies."[19] The abbey will, in fact, have its own stories and secrets, but they are not to be found in the trifling bits of paper she discovers.

In 2003, the *New York Times* reporter Lily Koppel realized a Catherine Morland-esque dream when she found a red leather diary in an old steamer trunk "strewn with vintage labels evoking the glamorous age of ocean liner travel" on New York's Upper West Side.[20] This long-forgotten tome traced the life of a woman named Florence Wolfson from the age of 14 in 1929 to the age of 19. The trunk, which was one among dozens languishing in the basement of a pre war building at 82nd Street and Riverside Drive, had been thrown into a dumpster, along with its compatriots, and Koppel, who lived in the building, came across them. She sounds very much like Catherine when she recounts the discovery:

> At first glance, I counted more than fifty trunks and elegant valises piled high like a magic mountain, just a polishing away from their descendants at Louis Vuitton. At the top, a tan trunk studded with brass rivets glowed in the sun with such luminescence that it appeared spotlit. With a copious skin of grand hotel labels, it betrayed its age like a sequoia."[21]

Koppel's discovery of the diary led to an article for the *Times* and a book—*The Red Leather Diary*—about not only

Wolfson's personal history, but the world of 1920s and 1930s New York City that she dutifully chronicled. The object itself was returned to Wolfson, who wrote a preface to the book.

These abandoned and neglected trunks were brought out of storage only to be thrown away; one wonders what else was lost. When the Willard Psychiatric Center in upstate New York closed in 1995, 427 suitcases filled with patients' belongings were found in the hospital's attic. Like the trunks on the Upper West Side, they might also have been thrown away. But several years later, Director of Recipient Affairs of the New York State Office of Mental Health Darby Penny began a ten-year project to go through the bags and recover the stories of their owners. Working with psychiatrist and documentary filmmaker Peter Stastny and photographer Lisa Rinzler, they collaborated to produce a 2004 exhibit at the New York State Museum and a book entitled *The Lives They Left Behind*. The suitcases became a way of accessing the lives of people who had been forgotten. Penny, Rinzler, and Stastny focused on ten patients, including a man named Lawrence Marek, who was admitted to the facility in 1916. His monogrammed calfskin valise contained two shaving mugs, two shaving brushes, and suspenders.[22]

When suitcases are lost, their secrets are lost, too. When Walter Benjamin crossed the Pyrennes in 1940 to flee the Nazis, he carried a suitcase with him. Lisa Fittko, his guide across the mountains who died in 2005, spoke of how he guarded this suitcase as if it contained a treasure. It may have contained a manuscript by Theodor Adorno. It may have contained his own final manuscript, but there is no mention of any manuscript in the judge's report of Benjamin's property. These items were: "A suitcase leather, a gold watch, a pipe, a passport issued in Marseilles by the American Foreign Service, six passport photos, an X-ray, a pair of spectacles, various magazines, a number of letters, and a few papers, contents unknown, and some money."[23] The secrets of that suitcase are the secrets of an exile. Indeed, luggage—or the absence of luggage—can mark us as divided from our homes in tragic ways. Exiled from Rome to "the Black Sea's sinister rocky shoreline",[24] Ovid writes that:

> I'd lacked time—and inclination—to get things ready,
> long procrastination had numbed my will:
> Too listless to bother with choosing slaves, attendants,
> the wardrobe, the outfit an exile needs.[25]

He sets off without a sense of what, or who, will come with him. The needs of an exile press upon him, but he is unable to summon the will to prepare. At a later point, he refers to, "books, my unlucky obsession, why do I stay with you/when it was my own talent that brought me down?"[26] This question may refer to the book of poems he is writing, but it also suggests that he brought books with him, a literary luggage loaded with the weight of exile.

Today, exiles may or may not be able to carry things with them. Artist and illustrator George Butler walked from Turkey across the border into Syria in August 2012, where as a guest of the rebel Free Syrian Army he drew what he saw of the civil war in the town of Azaz. He made another trip back six months later, again recording the stories of refugees in field hospitals. One of his illustrations depicts some of the belongings of one family during their time at a camp in Beqaa Valley, Lebanon.[27] The objects are not in a bag or a suitcase—they are simply scattered in empty space: photographs, a Dingling electric razor, scissors, and a notebook, the words floating out beyond the page. These placeless objects invoke displaced subjects. A 2017 exhibit at New York's Parsons School of Design entitled *State of Exception/Estado de Excepción* focused on the abandoned belongings of immigrants entering the United States from Mexico through Arizona's Sonoran Desert. In his review of the show, Holland Cotter notes that "from 2001 to 2009, at least 2,500 migrants died, and probably many more whose bodies vanished."[28] One gallery wall was covered with "dirt-caked backpacks of the kind seen in the entrance video. As if from inside the packs, taped voices emerge of migrants recounting desert ordeals."[29] The backpacks operate as not only as memorials for the dead, but also as witnesses. New York City's own immigration history can't be understood apart from the things that people brought with them—things they clung to and things they lost. The entrance to the National Museum of Immigration at Ellis Island in New York City is the Baggage Room, where immigrants checked their baggage before proceeding through inspection, and some of this luggage is on display in the museum.

Disasters leave luggage behind. Genocide leaves luggage behind. In David Foster Wallace's 1995 essay for *Harper's* about the absurdities of luxury cruises "A Supposedly Fun Thing I'll Never Do Again," the invisible handling of baggage brings to mind the Holocaust: "A second Celebrity crowd-control lady has a megaphone and repeats over and over not to worry about our luggage, that it will follow us later, which I am apparently alone in finding chilling in its unwitting echo of the Auschwitz-embarkation scene in *Schindler's List*."[30] Years ago, several suitcase towers were installed in the baggage claim area of the Sacramento airport, where I grew up. These towers comprised vintage suitcases—leather and hard-shell cases in various colors and sizes. I think these towers were supposed to be whimsical, something to look at in a flight-induced state of fatigue as you wait for your own bag to appear on the baggage carousel, but I always thought that they looked like a Holocaust memorial. They bring to mind not the inconvenience of a lost bag at an airport, but mass murder and its traces.[31] News footage of plane crashes is haunted by suitcases floating in the ocean or scattered on the side of a mountain. We do not see the people who died, but we often see their luggage. Eventually, some of this luggage may end up in a warehouse, catalogued and categorized. Other bags disappear, sink, or burn into nothingness. The luggage that went down with the *Titanic* on April 14 to 15, 1912, had been tagged as either "Wanted in Cabin" or "Not Wanted in Cabin." Those in Third Class might have traveled with only a carpetbag; those in First Class would have had trunks, some in their cabin and some stored in the ship's hold. If the ship had docked safely in New York City, this luggage would have been sorted by class, and alphabetically, and arranged on the dock to be collected. Instead, it became inhabited by sea creatures. The insurance claims filed by the survivors are the only traces of their lost possessions.

Sometimes luggage lost in disasters is found. In 2013, Pete Thomson, honorary curator of the Whitby Lifeboat Museum in the UK, purchased the trunk of a woman named Mary Roberts on eBay. Roberts had survived not only the *Titanic* (she worked as a stewardess and escaped on one of the lifeboats), but also the sinking of the *Rohilla* two years later. Her trunk, which was lost in the North Sea in that disaster, was listed by an antiques dealer in Lincolnshire, who agreed to sell it to the museum for 50 pounds.[32] According to a *New York Times* article from April 24, 1912, only one piece of luggage was saved from the *Titanic*:

> Of all the baggage that was on the White Star liner Titanic only one piece was saved. This was a carry-all, or canvas bag, belonging to Samuel L. Goldenberg, one of the saloon passengers rescued by the Carpathia. At the Custom House Special Deputy Surveyor George Smyth said that it was true that Mr. Goldenberg was the only passenger who saved any baggage, and that his carry-all was the only piece of luggage that was placed underneath any customs letter the night that the Carpathia arrived.[33]

The brown canvas bag, which was described as three feet high and two feet thick and filled with possessions, did not appear to have gotten wet at any point, and it was not clear how it had been transported from the *Titanic* to the *Carpathia*. It became something of a mystery, an almost mythic object. Today, the luggage company Chariot Travelware makes a hardside spinner suitcase with the rather macabre name "Titanic." It is designed to look like an old-fashioned suitcase, with a mock-leather body and straps.

The day starts out rainy but improves, the clouds burning away by the afternoon as we head into Georgia's green. The landscape brings to mind a color from the J.Crew catalog when I was a kid. I think it was called "Lawn," but it was not the color of a lawn—it was more brilliant, iridescent. This nineties color is the color of the hills as we drive the two-lane highways, the windows down, the air the air of spring.

I pull over at an antiques store with sign for GENUINE ANTIQUES . . . AND MAN STUFF TOO! It's closed, so I just look at the things on the front porch: old tin dishes and teapots, bottles and barrels, a red Escort train case, and an antler painted with a winter forest scene of quail by a frozen lake. I wish I could buy the antler. And maybe the train case. We drive around Lake Burton and past farms and churches and cemeteries, the graves marked with clean silk flowers.

The sun is setting as we pull up to the Heidi Motel in Helen. All of the motels along the main street are Bavarian-themed, including the chains. The sign for the Heidi depicts a little girl and her goat on a hillside, with a lake and a windmill in the background. And the motel has its own windmill. I roll down the windows and leave Millie in the car while I go into the office and ask if they're dog-friendly. They are. It's easy to find dog-friendly motels off the interstates. You learn which chains take pets, and then you can just pull off whenever you decide to quit for the evening. I tend to choose a Super 8 with a Cracker Barrel and a Waffle House close by, so dinner and breakfast are set. But I prefer old, quirky motels like this. They're just harder to find.

The woman behind the counter checks me in and gives me my key—an actual *key*, not a keycard—and says that the room on the second floor of the windmill is open, so I can have that one. I get my suitcase out of the car, and Millie and I walk up the steps on the back of the windmill. It's raining again. The base of the windmill is stone, lined with white twinkle lights, and the windmill itself is white wood. The plastic chairs by the door to my room have been tilted against the side of the building to keep them from gathering water.

Inside, I set my suitcase on floor, between the door and the gas fireplace, unzip it, and take out a sweater. I turn on the fireplace's timer, and the fire is nice on such a gloomy night, although it does make a clicking noise. Then I walk down the street to pick up dinner to go (a cheeseburger and a BLT) and chat with an older couple at the end of the bar while I wait for my food and drink my bourbon. I just want to sit by myself, but they are insistent in an affectionate, if slightly drunk, way—"How can you be by yourself? That's terrible. Come sit with us."—so I give up and scoot down a few chairs to talk to them. The husband asks me what I do, and I say that I'm an English professor.

"Good for you," he says.

I don't really know what to say to this, so I say thanks.

The bartender hands me my order, and I head back to the Heidi. I would watch HGTV, but the cable is out, so instead I *sit at the table by the window and look out over the rainy town. When a tourist town is not quite itself, when it's cold and dark and abandoned, you feel that you have been allowed to see something that other people don't get to see. Such melancholy nights in unreal places.*

2 THE LANGUAGE OF LUGGAGE

What do we mean by "luggage"? The word has its origins in war culture: for hundreds of years, it referred to the baggage, munitions, and supplies of an army, including trunks, backpacks, mess equipment, shoulder bags, and pouches suitable for a soldier, especially a cavalryman or an artilleryman. It was inconveniently heavy stuff that had to be lugged about. In Shakespeare's *Henry V*, the Welsh captain Fluellen expresses horror at a violent act of the French forces: "Kill the poys [boys] and the luggage! 'Tis expressly against the law of arms" (4.7.1).[1] These young victims were guarding the army's luggage at Agincourt. In Tim O'Brien's story "The Things They Carried," we learn about what a platoon of soldiers in Vietnam carries with them: not simply practical items, such as extra rations, weapons, and socks, but also letters and photographs. The story opens with some of these letters: "First Lieutenant Jimmy Cross carried letters from a girl named Martha, a junior at Mount Sebastian College in New Jersey. They were not love letters, but Lieutenant Cross was hoping, so he kept them folded in plastic at the bottom of his rucksack."[2] Carefully protected and stored away, these letters connect Lieutenant Cross, however tenuously, to his home and to a desired future. This story is about labor: the labor of carrying things that have both a real and a sentimental weight. To say that you "carry" something implies more of a burden than saying that you "brought" something with you. For the soldiers, the term is "hump": "To carry something was to hump it, as when Lieutenant Jimmy Cross humped his love for Martha up the hills and through the swamps. In its intransitive form, to hump meant to walk, or to march, but it implied burdens far beyond the intransitive."[3] These are the burdens of human relationships the burdens of attachments and memories. They are the burdens of desire, love, and hope. The letters are not simply letters: they are missives from beyond the war. This story reminds us that value is a complex thing. A pouch of rice may be valuable, as may a flak jacket or a groundsheet, and so the soldiers want those things, or need them. But for someone who is alienated from his home, surrounded by violence and faced with the possibility of death, other things take on a value that transcends utility. The story has the quality of an inventory: a list not unlike a packing list. This seemingly impersonal form allows the reader access not only to the interior of these rucksacks, but also to the interiority of the soldiers: their thoughts and memories and selves.

Today, "luggage" means all baggage that belongs to travelers and passengers, especially baggage that is transported by public conveyance. We often refer to our luggage as our "bags," collapsing it with other kinds of containers that hold our things and allow us to transport them. It is hard to think about life without bags. As Steven Connor notes, "Human beings make the world into bags, because holding things together, holding things up, and being ourselves held and held up, are so important to us."[4] Certainly the products made by Delsey, TravelPro, Tumi, Rimowa, Samsonite, Atlantic, American Tourister, and Rockland are luggage, but we carry our things around in all sorts of containers that may not be rolling suitcases. Is a backpack luggage? Perhaps a large one intended for outdoor adventures but not a small one intended for school. Shopping bags, tote bags, purses, briefcases, attaché cases, shoulder bags, fanny packs, camera cases, picnic baskets, cardboard boxes, garbage bags, guitar cases, ski bags—are these luggage? Is the 1960s green-and-blue tapestry Avon bag that Dianne Wiest's character Peg carries in *Edward Scissorhands* (1990) luggage? An antique book strap once allowed you to carry your books around, but it isn't a container or a bag. A corpse is a subject transformed into an object, so perhaps a body bag is luggage. Coffins are transported around the world in the cargo holds of commercial airplanes. They might be luggage. We speak of some luggage as "cargo," both for planes and ships. This category tends to be associated with commercial objects rather than personal ones, but we refer to the part of the plane that holds our personal luggage as the "cargo hold," a term that collapses this distinction. Paddington

Bear, who dates from 1958, has a luggage tag affixed to him that reads DARKEST PERU TO LONDON ENGLAND Via PADDINGTON Stn, and on the back is the handwritten request, *Please look after this bear.* So perhaps he is a bear, and perhaps he is luggage.

Perhaps luggage is anything that protects an object (or set of objects) and renders it portable. In the nineteenth century, portable libraries were delivered to lighthouses along the Eastern coast of the United States. These libraries, which were transported in wooden cases that resembled trunks or small bookshelves, provided much-needed relief for the keepers from the isolation and labor of the job. Logbooks from the period testify to the fact that lighthouse keepers worked almost constantly, through weekends and holidays. Any particular library might travel up the entire Atlantic Coast, stopping at all lighthouses along the way to loan books.[5] Portable objects such as this one are difficult to categorize. Jane Austen traveled with a portable mahogany writing desk, or writing box, that was likely a gift from her father the Reverend George Austen in 1794, when she was nineteen. (The desk has been in the collection of the British Library in London since 1999.) It has a side drawer, and the writing surfaces fold back to reveal compartments for manuscripts, inkpots, and writing implements. In the late 1790s, Austen was working on drafts of *Pride and Prejudice, Sense and Sensibility*, and *Northanger Abbey*—and as one critic says, she "learnt how to write on the hoof."[6] Writing desks were "highly desirable items, a form of state-of-the-art equipment in a world where improvement of roads and carriages meant that people were travelling more than ever before."[7] In the 2008 film *Miss Austen Regrets* about the last years of her life, her sister Cassandra helps her to pack the manuscript of *Emma* for a trip to visit her niece Fanny. Although here the novel-in-progress is packed with her clothes and not in the writing desk, this scene of packing speaks to Virginia Woolf's vision of Jane Austen in *A Room of One's Own* (1929). For Woolf, Austen was the only female writer who managed to work without such a space—without a room of her own. Whether at home or abroad, she wrote surrounded by the distractions of life. The writing desk is a box. It is a piece of furniture. And it is luggage. It enabled Austen to work and to travel, taking her out into the world she understood so well and then allowing her to write it all down. And once, it was almost lost. In a letter to Cassandra from October 24, 1798, Austen writes of the "little adventure" of the temporary loss of the writing desk, which she describes as containing "all my worldly wealth." The desk and some dressing boxes were accidentally placed in a chaise that they set off toward Gravesend, but a man was dispatched on horseback to rescue the items.[8] Luggage is not simply a suitcase or its contents. It is less a set of objects than an idea, a way of thinking about the things we carry with us in life and why. "Luggage" comes from the verb "to lug," which is probably of Scandinavian origin. As the *Oxford English Dictionary* notes, the Swedish verb *lugga* means to pull a person's hair. A somewhat aggressive idea. From the fourteenth to the nineteenth century, to "lug" also had the sinister connotation of teasing, worrying, or baiting someone or something—like a bear or a bull. Bear-baiting was a popular blood sport in Renaissance London, and some of the same playhouses that staged Shakespeare's plays also hosted these events, where a bear was chained to the stage and torn apart by dogs. This poor creature was *lugged*: he was an object in a spectacle of cruelty. In Shakespeare's *Henry IV, Part 1*, Falstaff says to Prince Hal, "'Sblood, I am as melancholy as a gib cat or a lugg'd bear" (1.2.74–5).[9] The comparison underscores the commonness of this violence; a castrated cat and a lugged bear are, for Falstaff, fairly similar creatures, and either one is a suitable comparison for his own humorous melancholia. You could lug a horse, in the sense of pulling or tugging at its bit, and you could lug liquor, or drink it. (In a similar vein, we say today that you take a "drag" on a cigarette.) Now, to lug something is to pull it along laboriously; the term underscores difficulty and strife.

And then there is baggage. Although we sometimes use the words "luggage" and "baggage" synonymously, each has its own implications. Like "luggage," "baggage" could refer to the equipment that armies dragged around with them. "Baggage" comes from the Old French *bagage*, which referred to property picked up for carriage. The verb *baguer* meant to tie up, bind, or truss up, and the noun form *bagues* designated bundles and packs. The term "bag" derives from the Early Middle English *bagge*; in Old Norse, which may be the origin of the English term, *baggi* was a bag, pack, or bundle. (For me, any mention of bundles brings to mind Miss Hannigan's paramour Mr. Bundles in the 1982 film *Annie*, whose vats of dirty, bundled laundry provide the perfect cover for Annie to flee the orphanage.) During the Reformation, "baggage" was rather colorfully applied to the rites and accessories of Roman Catholic worship. One sixteenth-century writer lambasts, "This Popyshe baggage of dumme ceremonies." The term also had a distinctly misogynist sense: "baggage" could be a disreputable and worthless woman, often one considered to lead an immoral life (not unlike the word "strumpet"). It also meant a silly, saucy, artful, or sly woman. In a related vein, an "old bag" is an unattractive old woman, possibly an old prostitute. In the sixteenth century, baggage could also be dirt, refuse, or rubbish—something corrupt or rotten, including a person. Baggage was trashy and nasty. Today, the word is commonly used in the United States to refer to the portable property of travel. We speak of "baggage claim" but the "lost luggage" office, suggesting that if you bags fail to appear, they are transformed from baggage to luggage. And with the word "baggage," we enter the realm of metaphor. Baggage refers not only to our actual burdens, but to our emotional ones, as well. With this usage, we draw not on the Renaissance sense of garbage, but another usage pertaining to important matters. In his *Essays*, Francis Bacon wrote, "I cannot call Riches better than the Baggage of Vertue." Here, the "Baggage of Vertue" is something to be desired above riches, something worthy and valuable, although perhaps difficult to bear. Baggage is linked to a sense of duty and to the weight of thought. But sometimes baggage has no figurative value. Perhaps Sisyphus's boulder is baggage: the ultimate burden that offers nothing but its own burden-ness. Sisyphus is always going somewhere; Sisyphus is never going anywhere. And some journeys may involve not luggage, but baggage. When Dante descends into the Inferno with Virgil as his guide, he brings nothing with him; it is not that kind of trip. His baggage is the baggage of witness: "To hear the cries of despair, and to behold ancient tormented spirits as they lament / In chorus the second death they must abide."[10] And this is certainly enough. Sometimes luggage becomes a way of imagining our emotional lives as apart from ourselves. In "ShallCross," the poet C. D. Wright writes of "my rolling bags of grief," bags that hold our most painful emotions—those emotions we sometimes cannot contain, or hold, ourselves.[11] And in Sinead Morrissey's poem "The High Window," the speaker refers to the classic secretary figure in a Raymond Chandler novel as having "a life so narrow, probably from the outset, / its pathetic little batch of dull effects / could fit inside one suitcase."[12] A life not even of things, but of "effects."

In the language of the self-help industry, our personal baggage tends to be associated with the past and understood to be liability and a problem. Sitting on the New York subway recently, I saw an advertisement for Clutter.com that asked, "Does he have baggage? We'll pick it up." This service relies on conventional understandings of romance as laden with the baggage of at least one person (and very possibly both people), and storage is jokingly offered as the solution. Actual material objects—always tricky in a small city apartment, of course—become emblems of your partner's past that must be managed, controlled, and possibly eliminated from sight. His baggage is not only a wagon-wheel coffee table. That can be stored. No, he brings with him cliché masculine baggage: he can't commit; he can't communicate; etc. But his flaws, his baggage, can be picked up and taken away. And so our complex humanity, our pasts, is transformed from potential tragedy into comedy—or at least into a bad joke.

We tend to speak of our baggage in a retrospective manner. It is what we bring with us from the past: memory and experience conceived of in negative terms, as something painful and hard to bear. It's difficult to imagine the contemporary self-help industry existing without the idea that we all have baggage with which we, and others, must reckon. This is an important part of how baggage is understood: it is not only your own. According to conventional wisdom, it is your responsibility to confess your baggage to others, perhaps shamefully, so they understand how your character has been shaped and know what they are facing. We are told to be wary of people who have too much baggage. Such a person is supposedly too much trouble, too emotionally taxing. A burden. Of course, the word is a cliché, so it has its own baggage; it is worn down by overuse.

We might ourselves be baggage. At the beginning of Agnieszka Holland's 1993 film of Frances Hodgson Burnett's *The Secret Garden*, piles of luggage are unloaded from the ship that brings the orphaned Mary Lennox back from India. While this work takes place, the droves of orphans from the earthquake (a cholera epidemic in the book) are also catalogued and processed. They are assigned numbers: Mary is #43. When the housekeeper Mrs. Medlock comes to collect her, she refers to the child as "a plain piece of goods." She is a burden—not even an English burden, but a foreign one. Baggage from abroad. Previously privileged and spoiled, Mary is now less valued and less valuable than the bags that fill the screen around her. In her poem "The Luggage," Constance Urdang writes:

> Travel is a vanishing act
> Only to those who are left behind.
> What the traveler knows
> Is that he accompanies himself,
> Unwieldy baggage that can't be checked,
> Stolen, or lost, or mistaken.[13]

We accompany ourselves; we are inextricably joined to ourselves. But we are also "unwieldy," a burden that can't be shed or cast aside. The traveler is a split self—he's accompanies herself—but these two selves are joined to one another. She is herself *and* a kind of suitcase that he's brings with her. Perhaps the "unwieldy baggage" is an essential self, beyond the physical, beyond the body that moves from one place to another. This idea resonates with the ghostly x-ray images of the inside of carry-on bags as you pass through airport security. I always try to look at the screen, curious about the shapes and shades of other people's hidden things, but the images bring to mind nothing so much as human bodies: an x-ray of someone's chest and an x-ray of his bag are not dissimilar. Indeed, the expression "bag of bones" reminds us that we may be no more than containers in which things are carried. The phrase tends to be applied to someone who is emaciated, and so it draws attention to the disconcerting reality of being able to see one's insides, or bones, from the outside.

But there are rosier visions of the human as luggage or baggage. In the 1989 film *Steel Magnolias*, Olympia Dukakis's Clairee says to Shirley MacLaine, "Ousier, you know I love you more than my luggage." When you leave someone, and they want to say that they will miss you, they say, "Put me in your suitcase and take me with you." It is an expression of intimacy, that someone wants to be with you, wants to be close to you. Tossed in among your things. They become a stowaway. No one else will know that they are packed among your clothes and shoes and a toothbrush. In his poem "Stowaway," Stanley Moss writes, "Aging, I am a stowaway in the hold of my being," a line that resonates with W. B. Yeats's famous vision in "Sailing to Byzantium" of man as "fastened to a dying animal."[14] For Yeats, we die because we are stuck with, or in, our dying bodies. Moss's vision is both physical and metaphysical. The aging body holds not only the aging self, but also perhaps a younger self: a stowaway self from the past. And the "hold" is one's being, selfhood itself, with all its legitimate and illegitimate cargo. Stowing away is transgressive. Unsanctioned. And, by extension, seductive. The small elevator in Paris's Le Dokhan's hotel is lined with antique Louis Vuitton wardrobe trunks, so you become a stowaway of sorts in this space. In an episode of *I Love Lucy*, Lucy needs to get a passport but can't find her birth certificate, so she practices stowing away in a trunk and gets stuck. Luggage can even stow away itself: the luggage brand Paravel makes a $275 collapsible suitcase called the Stowaway (with folded dimensions of 17.5"x7"x2.5" and unfolded dimensions of 17"x13"x6.5") and instructs you to "keep one tucked inside larger bags for overnight excursions or for when your hoarding tendencies get the best of you."

Luggage has other metaphors. We speak of "unpacking" an idea as examining it critically, and indeed the term appears in the title of one of the most cited reflections on the daily effects of white privilege, Peggy McIntosh's checklist "White Privilege: Unpacking the Invisible Knapsack." To "unpack" a concept is to attempt to parse out its various parts, its assumptions and implications, as one takes clothing out of a suitcase. The result is a sense of understanding as expansion: that what was previously folded up (and not entirely visible) has been revealed in its complete, unfolded state. English professors tend to use this term in the classroom. We are always asking for things to be unpacked. Unpacking a poem. Unpacking a word. Portmanteau words ask to be unpacked. As "porter" is French for "to carry," and "manteaux" is a cloak, the word brings to mind the act of packing: the bringing together of different things. In the nineteenth century, a portmanteau was a case that opened into two equal halves. A portmanteau word is formed by combining two or more words. It is what one critic calls a "linguistic supercontainer."[15] The portmanteau "derives from the fact that the same segments (letters, phonemes, syllables) can be combined in different ways to produce different meanings" and that its "effects are simultaneous, and . . . the result is an expansion of meaning even more extensive than that effected by the pun."[16] James Joyce's novel *Finnegans Wake* is known for its portmanteaux such as "shuit," which invokes a suit, shirt, and shoes simultaneously.

Dylan Thomas saw portmanteau words as part of his craft, which he discusses in his 1951 "Poetic Manifesto":

> What I like to do is to treat words as a craftsman does his wood or stone or what-have-you, to hew, carve, mould, coil, polish and plane them into patterns, sequences, sculptures, fugues of sound expressing some lyrical impulse, some spiritual doubt or conviction, some dimly-realised truth I must try to reach and realise. And I am a painstaking, conscientious, involved and devious craftsman in words . . . I use everything & anything to make my poems work and move in directions I want them to: old tricks, new tricks, puns, portmanteau-words, paradox, allusion, paronomasia, paragram, catachresis, slang, assonantal rhymes, vowel rhymes, sprung rhythm.[17]

In the list he presents, the term appears after "old tricks," "new tricks," and "puns," suggesting a cleverness to such combinations—even the sense that the reader is being fooled. In his *Apology for Poetry*, the first work of literary criticism in the English language, Sir Philip Sidney wrote that a poet does not simply represent or reflect the world, or hold a mirror up to nature (as Hamlet says). He *makes*. He invents. He creates something new that did not exist before. The fusing of words is one such making, and it generates something that is both familiar and strange. As invented words, portmanteaus are the embodiment of invention itself, of the act of writing.

Portmanteaus are related to "ghostwords," a term invented in the nineteenth century by editor W. W. Skeat, to describe words that don't exist or are mistakes, as well as "phantom words," which are errors or corruptions made by scribes or printers. Some of these words eventually enter the language, shedding their ghostly or phantomlike status. In Lewis Carroll's *Through the Looking-Glass*, Alice and Humpty-Dumpty discuss the portmanteau in "Jabberwocky." The opening stanza of the poem presents a series of portmanteaus, which Humpty-Dumpty defines as "two meanings packed into one word," drawing on the idea of packing:

> Twas brillig, and the slithy toves
>> Did gyre and gimble in the wabe:
> All mimsy were the borogoves,
>> And the mome raths outgrabe.[18]

In *The Raven and the Writing Desk*, Francis Huxley wrote of these lines that "occult meanings come thick and fast."[19] When questioned, Humpty-Dumpty informs Alice that "slithy" is both "lithe" and slimy" simultaneously (when I read the book as a kid, I thought it sounded like "slimy" and "slithering," too) and claims that "'*Brillig*' means four o'clock in the afternoon—the time when you begin broiling things for dinner." But some portmanteaus can't be defined in so straightforward manner. Humpty-Dumpty says, "Well, '*toves*' are something like badgers—they're something like lizards—and they're something like corkscrews," bringing together three disparate ideas that don't necessarily relate to the sound of the portmanteau but nonetheless account for its meaning. This conversation goes on for some time, with Alice asking what each word means, and Humpty-Dumpty outlining how they draw on the sounds or meanings of other words. The reader is left with the impression that meaning is associative: that we come to know what something is by knowing something else.

Portmanteau words defamiliarize language, rendering it strange, even as they are almost immediately, instinctually, recognizable for what they are. They ask us to think about how meaning works. Mary Ruefle's poem "Müller and Me" is an occasion to contemplate how a word's meaning might be determined by separating out the words that comprise it:

I am an ordinary fauna, one
who can't remember if a *fife*
is a *rifle* or a *flute*.
After all, there's *strife*
and *fight* in it,

but on the other hand
it's a short sweet word
that rhymes with *life*.[20]

Appropriately, a fife is neither a rifle nor a flute, but sort of a combination of the two: it is a military instrument, a flute that lives in a world of rifles. There is, therefore, strife and fight in it, as the narrator says, but there is also the question of rhyme "on the other hand," which suggests that this mystery will not be solved by thinking of "fife" as a portmanteau. Like rhyme, portmanteaus rely on the relationship between sound and meaning, but rhyme takes you away from a word, out of it, to another word.

In the introduction to *The Hunting of the Snark*, Carroll returns to Humpty-Dumpty's thoughts on these words: "Humpty Dumpty's theory, of two meanings packed into one word like a portmanteau, seems to me the right explanation for all. For instance, take the two words 'fuming' and 'furious.' Make up your mind that you will say both words, but leave it unsettled which you will say first . . . if you have the rarest of gifts, a perfectly balanced mind, you will say 'frumious.'" Here, Carroll focuses on order, reminding us that the portmanteau rearranges its words, or sounds, resulting in a balance like the "balanced mind" that produces it. Portmanteaus are about not having to choose which term is suited to what you want to say: you can say *both* words. If language is always about choice, the portmanteau liberates you, freeing you from this limitation. The term "Boojum" in *The Hunting of the Snark* is, according to Carroll, "a portmanteau formed out of a book-jack and boot-jam: and this last is obviously what happens when you cannot get whatever it is out of your boot (which is now on the other foot) even with the aid of the Jack of Hearts."[21] The playfulness of the term "obviously" hints at both the portmanteau's impenetrability and its clarity.

A person might be a portmanteau. Raoul Duquette, the narrator of Katherine Mansfield's 1920 story "Je Ne Parle Pas Francais," says:

> I don't believe in the human soul. I never have. I believe that people are like portmanteaux—packed with certain things, started going, thrown about, tossed away, dumped down, lost and found, half emptied suddenly, or squeezed fatter than ever, until finally the Ultimate Porter swings them on to the Ultimate Train and away they rattle.[22]

Like Mansfield herself, Duquette is an exile: a 26-year-old would-be poet living in Paris who says that he has no family and has forgotten his childhood. The story opens with his musings in (and on) a favorite café, where he imagines the transport of the clientele-as-portmanteaux through life and to death. In Raoul's humorous formulation, there is no ineffable self, no soul; one is simply "packed with certain things."[23] In this vision, he becomes a "Customs official" who asks, "Have you anything to declare? Any wines, spirits, cigars, perfumes, silks? And the moment of hesitation as to whether I am going to be fooled just before I chalk that squiggle, and then the other moment of hesitation just after, as to whether I have been, are perhaps the two most thrilling instants in life. Yes, they are, to me." Everyone is an exile, and they can deceive you.

If portmanteaus are words that hold things, books hold things, too. As Sergei Dovlatov writes in his novel/memoir *The Suitcase*, in which he chronicles the things he brought with him when he left the USSR in 1978, "There's a reason that every book, even one that isn't very serious, is shaped like a suitcase."[24] Books are suitcases for language. And indeed some suitcases actually contain words. T. E. Lawrence might have lost a suitcase containing the original manuscript of *The Seven Pillars of Wisdom* in Reading Station in 1919. But Lawrence may have burned the manuscript. The discovery in 1997 of a typescript of a version of the text, possibly from 1922, revived interest in the mystery. In 1922, a small valise filled with Ernest Hemingway's writing was stolen from Paris's Gare de Lyon. It contained his manuscripts—and the carbon copies of his manuscripts—that his first wife Hadley Richardson had packed to take with her to Lausanne, Switzerland, where Hemingway had been for several weeks. But she left the suitcase unattended for a moment before the train departed, and when she returned, it was gone. In January of the next year, Hemingway wrote to Ezra Pound about the loss:

I suppose you heard about the loss of my Juvenalia? I went up to Paris last week to see what was left and found that

Hadley had made the job complete by including all carbons, duplicates, etc. All that remains of my complete works are three pencil drafts of a bum poem which was later scrapped, some correspondence between John McClure and me, and some journalistic carbons. You, naturally, would say, "Good" etc. But don't say it to me. I ain't yet reached that mood. I worked 3 years on the damn stuff.

His combination of despair and levity speak to the difficulty of reckoning with the stolen suitcase. He also writes of it in *A Moveable Feast*, which was published posthumously in 1964:

I had never seen anyone hurt by a thing other than death or unbearable suffering except Hadley when she told me about the things being gone. She had cried and cried and could not tell me. I told her that no matter what the dreadful thing was that had happened nothing could be that bad, and whatever it was, it was all right and not to worry. We could work it out. Then, finally, she told me. I was sure she could not have brought the carbons too and I hired someone to cover for me on my newspaper job. I was making good money then at journalism, and took the train for Paris. It was true all right and I remember what I did in the night after I let myself into the flat and found it was true.[25]

There are two losses here, separated by his trip back to Paris: first, the loss of the suitcase, and secondly, the loss of the hope that the carbon copies might still be in their apartment. The manuscripts literally vanish without a trace as their traces are also gone. Hemingway had not yet been published when the suitcase was stolen, and this loss became an important part of his mythology and how his career was narrated and understood: as predicted on absence, on non-pages. And this is a story not only about lost manuscripts, but also about the displacement that defined the community of expatriate writers in Paris at the time. It is about travel and the materials of travel. One wonders what became of the suitcase's contents. Presumably the thief was disappointed with what he found. Perhaps he destroyed the pages. Perhaps he threw them away. Perhaps he kept the suitcase, and it is still out there somewhere, in a closet or under a bed.

In his 2006 Nobel Prize lecture, Orhan Pamuk spoke about his father's writing. His father had kept this work to himself for many years, but then, one day, he handed it over to Pamuk in a suitcase: "We were in my study, surrounded by books. My father was searching for a place to set down the suitcase, wandering around like a man who wished to rid himself of a painful burden. In the end, he deposited it quietly, unobtrusively, in a corner."[26] Surrounded by books, Pamuk reckons with what he calls the "mysterious weight" of a suitcase filled with notebooks that never became books, notebooks that represent the creative output of his father. He recognizes the "small black leather case, with a lock and rounded corners," and he remembers that when he was a child, his father had carried documents to and from work in it. He is afraid to open the suitcase and read his father's writing—afraid of what it will reveal about what it means to be a writer and what it means to be happy. Pamuk thinks of his father as happy. But happiness has been, for him, harder to attain. The suitcase mediates a relationship between the two men and between different ways of being in the world.

But the suitcase is not only an emblem of a loving but fraught relationship between father and son. It also tells a story about exile, both geographic exile—Pamuk's sense that he was "living in the provinces, far from the center of things" in Istanbul—and the sense of exile that a writer feels, shut away from the world. The suitcase smells of travel. His father spent time away from his family, in Paris, writing. And he brought books back with him. The suitcase holds evidence of another side of this affable and social man. It reveals his discontent, which Pamuk sees as "the basic trait that turns a person into a writer." In the suitcase are the hidden thoughts, and words, that discontent gives rise to:

> As I gazed at my father's suitcase, it seemed to me that this was part of what was causing me disquiet after working in a room, trying to survive as a writer in Turkey for twenty-five years, I was galled to see my father hide his deep thoughts in this suitcase, to see him act as if writing were work that had to be done in secret, far from the eyes of society, the state, the people.

The suitcase hides a self that created "new worlds," as writers do. When he speaks about reading his father's notebooks, he speaks about the difficulty of memory: "What had my father written about? I recall a few views from Paris hotels, a few poems, paradoxes, analyses. . . . As I write, I feel like someone who has just been in a traffic accident and is struggling to remember how it happened, while at the same time dreading the prospect of remembering too much." They never discuss the notebooks.

I get up early the next morning so I have time to walk around town before heading to Atlanta. I want to go to the souvenir shops. Most people think that souvenirs are junk, but I love them. Cheap material memories, both beautiful and ugly— empty nothings charged with meaning. I take Millie for a walk and then leave her lounging on the bed in the motel room and head down the stairs and out of my windmill. The housekeepers are working in the rooms in one of the main buildings, and we say hello. I don't think there are many other occupied rooms.

I walk down the motel's drive, to the town's main street, and turn left, toward the shops and restaurants. In the distance, behind several Alpine-themed chain motels—maybe a Hampton Inn?—is the river, which looks quiet and sad. I walk past a museum called Charlemagne's Kingdom (closed). A pickup truck drives by with a taxidermy polar bear on the back. A block ahead, the truck stops at a light, so I pick up my pace to catch up with it. Two men unload the bear and set it down on the sidewalk. His paw is outstretched, and he's fighting a badger. The bear's fur has been messed up and needs to be smoothed down. It's drizzling, and I'm worried that he'll get wet. The men pick him up and carry him into an alleyway, and he's gone.

I walk into a store that sells wooden shoes of all sizes: actual wooden shows and miniatures and magnets of wooden shoes. The walls are lined with wooden shoes. I buy some of the miniatures. Across the street is a store that specializes in cuckoo clocks. I pick out a few fridge magnets: beer steins, blonde children kissing each other with "Helen, GA" emblazoned below them, a Viking ship, a Russian nesting doll. A couple of cuckoo clocks. Quite a mix. I figure that I'll add a few to my collection at home and give a few away. I decide on a snow globe, too, and take everything up to the counter. The older man behind the counter has been chatting with the two other customers in the shop, and he seems to be the owner. The other people leave, and he turns to me. We have some small talk about the rain and my magnet choices.

"I'll have to come back one day and get an actual clock," I say.

"Yes," he says.

Back at the motel, I wrap the magnets up in my clothing and stash them away in my suitcase, on the road-tripping side. I don't change into work clothes; I leave that side of the suitcase zipped for now. I'll change when I get there. I drag the suitcase back down the stairs, out of the windmill, and load it in the car. Millie jumps in.

Then: Atlanta.

3 PACKING

Packing is the first step of travel—if this travel is deliberate, if it is something you choose to do. Travel is in part defined by its deliberateness, or purposefulness. This is what makes it different from other ways that we move through space. Different from a tragedy, such as being forced to leave your home, or different from something utterly ordinary, like going to work every morning, even if you live far from where you work (this is still referred to as a commute, not a trip or a journey). Travel has been characterized as "all passage across significant boundaries that separate differing personas, kinds of social relations, activities."[1] When you travel, you are choosing to leave your home behind. And your luggage, your suitcase more often than not, is the distillation of the domestic, abroad: your home, reduced. This is what we mean by "living out of a suitcase."

Writing of his parents in the 1940s, Richard Ford recalls that his salesman father, who traveled for work during the week, never unpacked when he came home:

Most always, he was not there—my father. Though I remember his Ford sitting at the curb on weekends, remember the sound of him in the house, in the bathroom, snoring in his bed. I remember the size of him. His never unpacked. His change, wallet, pocket-knife, handkerchief, and watch were on his bed table (they did not sleep together anymore).[2]

His personal effects grounded him at home, if only temporarily, but the suitcase is a reminder that he is perpetually traveling, always already gone. Ford writes of the closeness between his mother and father, which was forged by traveling together early in their marriage—a life on the road, just the two of them—but when Ford was born, she stayed home. The parentheses ("they did not sleep together anymore") don't necessarily signal an unhappy or strained marriage, but a change in how things were that he also felt in the perpetual presence of the leather suitcase.

Our suitcases mark us as displaced, as lacking a home and, by extension, the closets and drawers that contain our possessions. Our luggage holds the objects we choose to take with us, what we think we will need. And choosing these things—packing—is an exercise in anticipation, in imagining the unknown and attempting to account and prepare for it. Is it likely to rain? You may need an umbrella. Will you need practical shoes? Dressy shoes? Perhaps both. Some people makes lists of what they want to pack, so as not to forget anything. Forgetting to pack something is an anxiety fundamental to travel. Hotels and motels register this anxiety with signs at the check-in desk and even in the bathroom in your room that ask, "Forgot something?" and then assure you that the hotel has a (limited, seemingly arbitrary) selection of items on hand to replace what you left behind: razors, toothbrushes, etc. If the miniature hotel toiletries set out on a tray anticipate that you have left certain items behind because you know they will be provided, these signs about forgotten amenities remind you that you are an imperfect packer and, by extension, an imperfect traveler. You are defined by lack.

Suitcases ask to be filled. They are defined by their emptiness or fullness, their status as receptacles that shift between these two states. If a trip is long, or to a place far away, we might be more likely to make a list of what we think we'll need; the fear of forgetting something weighs heavily on us. Maybe we write these lists down, or maybe we hold them in our heads. Some people barely think about what they pack, and for others it is a charged ritual governed by rules and habits that are years in the making. One of my friends wraps her clothing in tissue paper and places some garments in Ziploc bags. The latter is a practice I have only adopted with regard to wet bathing suits. I remember thinking years ago that this must take forever, but later it occurred to me that this was part of the point: that she liked the process and the precision of it. Another friend rolls all of her clothes, carefully arranging them in neat stacks. I know couples who pack in the same suitcase (one large one instead of two smaller ones) and couples who would never dream of such a thing. Packing is about arranging objects in relationship to one another, fitting them together like a puzzle.

Packing is about inclusion and exclusion. You might lay your clothing out on your bed and look it over. But first you have to decide what size of bag or suitcase you're bringing with you. The right size. The right weight. The right kind of compartments. Are you flying or driving? Checking a bag or not? Can you take more than one bag? We sometimes speak of people as good or bad packers, and this value judgment concerns how effectively someone determines what he or she needs. Today, packing light tends to be considered good packing, and a seasoned traveler is identifiable by the deftness with which she manages her luggage. (Think of flight attendants marching through airport terminals, their black rolling suitcases behind them, a small black bag strapped to the top of each one.) Some adventures require a lot of luggage and others require almost nothing. At the beginning of *On the Road*, Jack Kerouac writes of his departure, "So, leaving my big half-manuscript sitting on top of my desk, and folding back my comfortable home sheets for the last time one morning, I left with my canvas bag in which a few fundamental things were packed and took off for the Pacific Ocean with fifty dollars in my pocket."[3] His canvas bag is suited to traveling by bus and to hitchhiking, and its contents hardly matter: they are simply "fundamental things," a phrase that resonates with the romantic goals of his trip out West.

You don't really know if you have packed well until you arrive at your destination. After a day or so, or after a rainstorm, or after an unexpected invitation that requires a particular kind of clothing: this is when the quality of your packing becomes clear. This is when you know what you have and what you lack. And indeed, there is an entire industry that reminds us, or convinces us, that packing is difficult and stressful and then provides guidance and advice. Magazines like *Martha Stewart Living* and *Real Simple* publish endless articles about packing, sometimes including packing lists that can be adapted to your needs. Such checklists are tailored to different kinds of vacations—"Beach Vacation Packing List" and "Ski Trip Packing List"—and often divide your packing "essentials" into categories (Accessories, Clothing, Equipment, Health and Beauty Items, etc.) that create a further sense of order and organization. There are even videos to help you with the process, in case you want to watch every step performed. Wondering how to pack for your beach honeymoon? You have only to turn to *Real Simple* for a list of clichés. Don't forget lingerie, a travel candle "with a romantic scent" (not pine, presumably?), bubble bath, and scented massage oil. And contraception. The "Add-On" section for a beach honeymoon reminds you that you should bring aloe vera gel or after-sun cream, a sun hat, and a second swimsuit and cover-up. You should also bring "paperbacks," presumably because they are lighter than hardback books, but the term also suggests a frivolous women's "beach read."[4] These are not books; books are heavy, in both weight and content. These are just paperbacks.

According to the packing industry, packing is not a banal activity, but a specialized skill that can be learned. The industry draws heavily on the language and ideology of the self-help industry, promising that mastering this skill will make you a better and happier person. And packing mastery tends to involve consumption: there is always a better suitcase out there for our needs, always a more efficient bag in which to arrange our toiletries. Pack-It Compressor bags by Eagle Creek, which create more space in your bag, are frequently recommended. These bags allow you to pack more than you normally would while simultaneously assuring you that you are packing in a streamlined and efficient manner. In a more luxurious vein, the section "What To Pack" from the destination travel, lifestyle, and fashion publication *Suitcase* is divided into the somewhat odd categories HOT, COLD, CITY, ACTIVE, and 100ML (the last category is beauty products), and you can purchase all of the items in each category. The luggage brand Away not only claims to manufacture "the perfect suitcase," but also inspires consumer desire by offering you access the packing practices of fashionable, creative jet-setters in the series "Unzipped" on their site *The Upgrade*. The series asks, "Ever stood at baggage claim wondering what was inside someone else's suitcase? Here's your answer." Each entry—"Unzipped in Wisconsin," "Unzipped in France," etc.—is a list of the traveler's essentials and a photograph of the contents of their open Away suitcase. From Malin+Goetz products to $89 striped J.Crew T-shirts, anything that is available for purchase is linked to the relevant website so you, too, can buy it and put it in *your* suitcase.

"Travel experts" and "travel insiders" such as flight attendants often offer tips about how to pack an ideal suitcase. Such insiders promise access to information known only by members of an elite club, and the reader can aspire to belong to such a cabal and to know its "secrets." Advice tends to fall into two categories: the obvious (don't pack fabrics that are likely to wrinkle; put what you will need first on top) and the baffling (put dryer sheets between layers of clothing to "keep everything fresh"). The genre of obvious advice also extends to suitcase selection. Want your suitcase to stand out on the carousel?—By a bag in a bright color rather than black. But ideas about what constitutes good packing are overwhelmingly normative: they rely on an understanding that everyone needs more or less the same things when they travel. Eccentric packing is a sign of character, as it tends to eschew the practical and to disrupt expectations of what is required for a given trip. But we can't all be eccentrics nor, according to the packing industry, should we aspire to such a thing.

The good packer is a soothsayer: she can see into the future and anticipate what will be required. Her perfectly organized suitcase becomes an emblem of her perfectly organized life, as well as a sign of her control over the unpredictability of travel. I say "her" as the industry overwhelmingly targets women. It relies on, and often bolsters, misogynist cultural clichés of women as bad packers—as requiring and desiring too much when they travel. Sometimes this character flaw is class-bound. In Mel Brooks's 1987 film *Spaceballs*, the Princess Vespa (Daphne Zuniga) travels with not only matched luggage, a sign of privilege, but comically enormous matched luggage. Laden with her floral-printed bags, Barf the sidekick-dog refers to it disdainfully as *"Her Royal Highness's matched luggage!"* In fact, one of the cases holds a huge Claes Oldenburg-esque hair dryer: the ultimate emblem of female vanity. Likewise, when Phyllis Nefler (Shelley Long) goes camping with her Girl Scout troop in the 1989 comedy *Troop Beverly Hills*, they bring with them yellow-and-white striped matched luggage by Giorgio Beverly Hills. They are not about to rough it. Packing too much may also be a sign that you are becoming too female. In the 1959 cross-dressing classic *Some Like It Hot*, Jack Lemmon's character Daphne's overstuffed suitcase demonstrates that Lemmon's male self, Jerry, is morphing into a clothes-obsessed woman. An obnoxious 2010 headline in the *Daily Mail* proclaimed: "No surprises there then: Women DO pack too much when they go on holiday," citing research commissioned by www.travelsupermarket.com.[5] But perhaps the most efficient packer ever was Grace Kelly in *Rear Window* (1954), whose elegant and compact Mark Cross case contained only a white negligee for her overnight stake-out with Jimmy Stewart.

Efficient packing is the subject of numerous self-help-esque books. Kathleen Ameche's *The Woman Road Warrior: A Woman's Guide to Business Travel* includes advice on "how to pack the perfect suitcase." Susan Foster's *Smart Packing for Today's Traveler* and Anne McAlpin's *Pack It Up: Travel Smart, Pack Light* (with DVD) also promise efficient perfection. Fodor's has *How To Pack*, and Lonely Planet publishes *How To Pack for Any Trip*. Hitha Palepu's *How to Pack* even *looks* portable. Designed to resemble a suitcase trimmed in brown leather and affixed with a luggage nametag, this slim volume informs the reader that "it's time to pack perfect. Every trip, every time. Your journey starts here." Here, packing is folded into travel (no pun intended). It is part of your "journey," one of the self-help industry's favorite terms. The subhead—"Travel Smart for Any Trip"—also points to the book's expansive sweep: it will prepare you for *all trips*. The confident assertion on the back cover that "what and how you pack are who you are" represents the ideology of self-help at its most potent: packing is an extension of the self, and to do it badly is to be bad. Your character is not an ineffable thing; it is bound up in how well you perform the banal activities of life. Indeed, the first step of this "crash course" is for the reader to identify her "Packing Personality." The good news is that packing is an activity worthy of Picasso: it is not simply a skill, but an art ("The Art of the Perfectly Packed Suitcase").

The book's maxims tend to the grandiose, as if you were building Rome rather than rolling up your T-shirts and stuffing your socks into your shoes: "Anything worth achieving requires preparation," the reader is informed.[6] The eight tear-out-and-personalize packing lists at the end of the book ask you to map out your "outfits" for a five-day trip, both a.m. and p.m. Completing these lists, which the author refers to as her "trade secrets," is the culmination of your instruction, although the reader is informed that perfection is not easily achieved: "My streamlined method will be challenging at first (don't necessarily expect to pack lightly the first time you try), but push yourself to edit as much as possible. As you get more confident in your packing skills, you will find the process incredibly satisfying." *Incredibly satisfying*. Of course, this is the heart self-help. The goal is not simply a good trip, which is easily achieved by any number of people, but a temporary sense of profound happiness. This happiness comes with achieving packing perfection. But of course such a thing is impossible. The traveler can never anticipate everything, know everything, prepare for everything, include everything. It's the rare traveler who never wishes that she had brought a particular object with her; packing is about knowing that you will miss the home you left behind as you rummage through its traces in your bag.

Packing advice tends to be haunted by the specter of waste. Waste is a horror: you must not waste space. You must not bring anything unnecessary. Luggage is always about limitation—there is no such thing as an infinite suitcase. When my mother walked the Camino a few years ago, she had to choose what to carry with her in her pack.

Some people start the pilgrimage with too many things and shed them along the way. Before she left, she walked around Sacramento with her pack on her back to make sure that the things she carried with her were the right things; she took things out and put others in. And then she went to Spain with the right things. The poet Alice Oswald writes of the contents of her pack for her walk along the River Dart in Devon:

> In walking boots, with twenty pounds on my back: spare socks, compass, map, water purifier so I can drink from streams, seeing the cold floating spread above the morning,
>
> tent, torch, chocolate, not much else.
>
> Which'll make it longish, almost unbearable between my evening meal and sleeping, when I've got as far as stopping, sitting in the tent door with no book, no saucepan, not so much as a stick to support the loneliness.[7]

The long period of loneliness is measured in an absence of things—in things she does not have with her, a non-inventory. Sitting in the threshold space of the tent door, she feels a series of *no*'s, things that are not. Her finite pack is defined not only by what it holds, but also by what it does not. The French philosopher Roland Barthes has something to say about finite spaces. In his essay "The Nautilus and the Drunken Boat," he writes of Jules Verne's fantasy of reducing and enclosing the world:

Verne had an obsession for plenitude: he never stopped putting a last touch to the world and furnishing it, making it full with an egg-like fullness. His tendency is exactly that of an eighteenth-century encyclopedist or of a Dutch painter: the world is infinite, the world is full of numerable and contiguous objects. . . . Verne in no way sought to enlarge the world by romantic ways of escape or mystical plans to reach the infinite: he constantly sought to shrink it, to populate it, to reduce it to a known and enclosed space, where man could subsequently live in comfort: the world can draw everything from itself; it needs, in order to exist, no one else but man.[8]

For Barthes, Verne is obsessed with the idea of closure—a ship, for example, is one "emblem of enclosure," a thing that stands not just for departure, but for a desire to create a habitat that is finite. (Arthur Rimbaud's poem "The Drunken Boat" was influenced by Verne's *Twenty Thousand Leagues Under the Sea*.) This is the fantasy: that you can take everything with you when you depart. You don't have to choose one thing over another. You don't have to leave your home behind. You can recreate it, in all its fullness and completeness, elsewhere. He also argues that Verne's understanding of seclusion is linked to childhood:

Imagination about travel corresponds to an exploration of closure, and the compatibility between Verne and childhood does not stem from a banal mystique of adventure, but on the contrary from a common delight in the finite, which one also finds in children's passion for huts and tents: to enclose oneself and to settle, such is the existential dream of childhood and of Verne.[9]

This love of the finite—the hut or the tent—is no less than a way of "re-invent[ing] the world."[10] Writing of enclosed worlds like Joseph Cornell's glass bells, the island of Lilliput in *Gulliver's Travels*, and doll houses, Susan Stewart notes that

> the major function of the enclosed space is always to create a tension or dialectic between inside and outside, between private and public property, between the space of the subject and the space of the social. Trespass, contamination, and the erasure of materiality are the threats presented to the enclosed world.[11]

A suitcase marks the boundary between inside and outside, private and public. Stewart's understanding of enclosed worlds is darker than Barthes's: they are threatened by trespass and contamination, their boundaries can be breached—and of course this is true of a suitcase. This enclosed world can be disrupted, taken apart. But as Barthes notes, the enclosed world is also a space of imagination: "Imagination about travel corresponds to an exploration of closure." The child's imagination is fueled by spaces that promise to contain all of our needs and desires and to leave us lacking nothing.

One figure achieves this. A freedom from lack is part of Mary Poppins's self-proclaimed perfection in the 1964 Disney film: her carpet bag is infinite. It contains all of her desires. At the beginning of the film, we see that the bag is heavy enough to sink through the clouds as she sits above a surreal blue London, powdering her nose, but like her animated umbrella, it is also a powerfully enabling object. Mary Poppins does not have a home that she has left behind. She belongs to the elements, witch-like and free. When she arrives at the Banks's house and surveys her Spartan living arrangements, she immediately determines what is missing and produces these things from her bag. As the wide-eyed Jane and Michael look on, she unpacks a lamp and a large gilded mirror in which she gazes approvingly at her own reflection. Michael looks into the bag and then slides under the table to see where these things are coming from, but he is unable to solve the mystery. He sees only vacancy. He can't know the magic of the bag because the bag is not his. It belongs to his mysterious nanny, and it is her ownership of it, in part, that generates its magic. *The world is infinite, the world is full of numerable and contiguous objects*. Her carpet bag is all the objects of the world, contained in a finite space.

The scene plays out slightly differently in P. L. Travers's novel, where Mary Poppins is even more of a conjurer. The children establish that the bag is, in fact, *empty*, before she draws items out of it:

By this time the bag was open, and Jane and Michael
    were more than surprised to find it was completely
    empty.

"Why," said Jane, "there's nothing in it!"

"What do you mean—nothing?" demanded Mary
    Poppins, drawing herself up and looking as though
    she had been insulted. "Nothing in it, did you say?"

And with that she took out from the empty bag a
    starched white apron and tied it round her waist.
    Next she unpacked a large cake of Sunlight Soap, a
    toothbrush, a packet of hairpins, a bottle of scent, a
    small folding armchair and a box of throat lozenges.

Jane and Michel stared.

"But I saw," whispered Michael. "It *was* empty."[12]

Although she shushes the children and then administers
their delicious medicine, she's not able to squelch the sense
of wonder they feel in the presence of this carpet bag. Most
of the things that Mary Poppins travels with are luxuries.
They relate to her own grooming and encode her not as a
desperate figure of need, as is so often the case in representing
governesses like Jane Eyre in nineteenth-century fiction, but
as an autonomous woman able to produce whatever she wants.
The carpet bag represents a self-sufficiency that borders on
the autoerotic: Mary Poppins can please herself. The fact that
she travels light is also linked to her freedom. She can come
and go as the wind changes, which would hardly be possible

with a steamer trunk. At the end of the book, she leaves on the "wild west wind" with hardly a backward glance: "Mary Poppins was in the upper air now, floating away over the cherry-trees and the roofs of the houses, holding tightly to the umbrella with one hand and to the carpet bag with the other."[13] If there is a cruelty to this iconic character, it is the cruelty of all travelers: the restless spirit of the wanderer, the desire for pastures new. The desire to leave.

In the nineteenth century, carpet bags allowed you to transport essentials that you wanted to keep close to yourself. In Verne's *Around the World in Eighty Days,* Passepartout and Phileas Fogg's carpet bag contains clothing and money. Although *Mary Poppins* was published in 1934, it is set over twenty years earlier, so her carpetbag is a nostalgic object. That these bags were made of carpet linked them to the domestic sphere: the material invokes an idea of home even as it reminds the traveler that she is not at home. In fact, the material was remaindered Brussels carpet and "Oriental" rugs. Carpet bags were not heavy. This sense of lightness is an important feature of Anne Shirley's carpetbag in Lucy Maud Montgomery's 1908 novel *Anne of Green Gables.* Far from Mary Poppins's infinite bag, Anne's carpetbag represents a darker kind of placenessness rooted not in potential, but in the limitations of poverty. Hers is the placelessness of the unwanted orphan who is shuffled about from one "home" to another, all of these "homes" lacking the essential characteristics of a home, lacking a sense of belonging. But this bag, which is almost empty—which is, in a sense, *not packed*—plays an important role in the moment she meets the almost-silent Matthew Cuthbert: "Matthew, however, was spared the ordeal of speaking first, for as soon as she concluded that he was coming to her she stood up, grasping with one thin brown hand the handle of a shabby, old-fashioned carpetbag; the other she held out to him."[14] Her two hands—one on the bag, the other in his—represent her transition from orphan to daughter. She holds her bag; he holds her hand. That the carpet bag is "old-fashioned" underscores its status as inherited; it is not something she wanted or chose, and not something intended for her, like the objects that Matthew will give her over the years.

When he takes the bag from her, her personal connection to it becomes clear: "'Oh, I can carry it,' the child responded cheerfully. 'It isn't heavy. I've got all my worldly goods in it, but it isn't heavy. And if it isn't carried in just a certain way the handle pulls out—so I'd better keep it because I know the exact knack of it. It's an extremely old carpetbag.'"[15] She resists letting go of the bag. It is hers, and only she knows how to handle it. Anne says to Matthew that "I've never belonged to anybody—not really," and belonging in the novel is about ownership and possession: Anne wants nothing more than to belong to someone and somewhere—to be cared for, valued, and protected. She possesses almost nothing, but she wishes to be possessed herself.[16] In the 1985 television adaptation with Megan Follows, an even more intimate relationship between subject and objet is established as Anne notes that the bag is "thin and light" like her and then reflects on whether it is the sort of bag that the Lady of Shalott would carry, thus linking it to the poem that is central to her imaginative life. Unlike Mary Poppins, Anne has nothing, but if her bag is materially empty, it reminds us of her own imaginative capacity, her ability to call things forth—not literally, as Mary Poppins does, but figuratively. The world she envisions through books becomes her own mode of conjuring, and as she can place herself in the role of the Lady of Shalott (and will actually attempt to do so, in a leaky boat), so can she imagine a future that is different from her past and different from the almost-empty bag she clutches in her hand.

Academic conferences tend to be held at big corporate hotels. You could be anywhere. Boston. Tucson. New York. San Francisco. Atlanta. It doesn't matter. Once you walk into the hotel, you are in the world of the conference, and sometimes there are other conferences going on at the same time, so everyone looks like they're working, and you can tell which group someone belongs to by his or her nametag.

But the Hyatt Regency Atlanta, my home for the next three days, turns out to be surprisingly non-generic. The building was designed by John C. Portman, who is also known for the Westin Bonaventure Hotel in Los Angeles, where I attended another conference years ago. With its central atrium and rooms all around, the Hyatt Regency recalls Jeremy Bentham's eighteenth-century idea of the Panopticon, a circular institutional prison design with an inspection house at the center that allowed inmates to be observed by a watchman. The watchman was invisible, so the inmates didn't know when they were being watched and had to assume they were being watched at any moment. This watching controlled their behavior. There is no central inspection house here at the hotel. But still.

My room is 818. I roll my suitcase into the glass elevator, which soars up through the atrium, and then walk along the hallway, with its low walls and plants. I can see around, across, and right down. The place reminds me of the library when I was in grad school at NYU, which was beautiful, but it also felt haunted because a couple of students jumped one year.

Inside, I put my suitcase on the floor by the bathroom and open it up and contemplate what to take out and what to leave *for now. I hang some of my clothes in the closet, on those hotel hangers that have miniature hooks, presumably so you don't take them home with you. And I lay some of my clothes out on bed, thinking about what I should put on. I leave the road-trip-clothes side of the suitcase zipped. Then I unfold a hand towel on the counter in the bathroom and set my toiletries out on it. I feel settled, or as settled as one can feel in a hotel.*

I have a recurring anxiety dream that I'm supposed to give a paper in a hotel like this one, but I can't find the right room. I run from level to level, in and out of ballrooms and conference rooms, panicked. Sometimes someone who works at the hotel tries to help me, but it's no use: the room doesn't exist or he has never heard of it ("Salon A, you say? No, I haven't ever seen a Salon A."). I never make it to the session. I stay lost. I always think of this dream when I'm at a conference, like the dream wants to be real.

I was just at another conference in Chicago a week ago, so I'm feeling weary. It rained the whole time there, too, and I could hear the wind in the vent in my bathroom. A steady moan coming from somewhere deep in the hotel. This room has a balcony and a view out over downtown. I change into a skirt, a sweater, heels. Put on lipstick. Earrings. It's already the early evening—the drive into town took longer than I thought, and I had to drop Millie off at her boarding place—so I go downstairs to the lobby bar. Because that is what you do at a conference.

4 MY LUGGAGE

Although I have collected vintage luggage for a decade, I have only found one thing in an old suitcase: a painting of a house. I bought the olive-green hardside case (the smaller of two) at a consignment store in Winston-Salem, and when I opened it at home, I found the painting. I don't know if the suitcases belonged to the woman who made the painting, but I know that her name was M. E. Redman as this is how she signed her work:

> My old home—built 1889—
>   burned 1938—
>   Painted—M. E. Redman—1959

The back of the paper is mottled with a pale brown that is darkest where the color is most saturated on the front; it resembles a negative, an imprecise outline of the painting itself. The painting has the texture of oil pastels or paint. I can feel the colors under my fingers. The edges of the paper are cracked from age, and there is a crease across the upper left-hand corner that has been flattened out but is still visible. The

FIGURE 3

house itself is surrounded by trees on both sides, five on the left and four on the right, and the walkway that leads to the front door is lined with bushes. In the foreground is a fence, just in front of the walkway. The house is painted head-on, asserting its presence and its permanence, even as something that is gone. The yellowish curtains are pulled back from the windows, reminding you that this house has an inside, too, but that this interior is beyond the painting, beyond what you can see. *My old home*, she wrote. I wonder if the house was in Winston-Salem or if the suitcases somehow found their way here. I wonder if M. E. Redman worked from a photograph or from memory. She painted her house twenty years after it burned down, but perhaps she still remembered it. Maybe she was born here and lived here all of her life. Or maybe she bought the house as an adult and didn't live in it very long. In either case, she lost her house and, possibly, her possessions. The painting is a memorial. And now it is in a suitcase: her house has been relegated to a suitcase, where it rests on stained olive-green quilted padding. As a friend said to me, it is almost too much—if this showed up in a novel, you would say: no. No way. *Built 1889, burned 1938, painted 1959.* Time, mapped out by a house. I bought a frame for M. E. Redman's painting, and now it hangs in my house. Perhaps I should have left it in the suitcase. Perhaps it lives there. But I don't think so.

It is appropriate that I should find a house that no longer exists in a brand of suitcases that no longer exists. These Airway suitcases are particularly satisfying to close, as the angled clasps open to the side—so you push them in to close the case, not down, as on many mid-century Samsonites. When you press the top down, there is the first click, the sense of something being closed. If you simply let the top of the case drop, it catches on the edge of the clasps, but it doesn't quite close. Thus closing the suitcase is something you *have* to do, an effort and a process that results in a sealed thing, a thing that holds other things apart from the world. Suitcases with zippers don't create this sense of security. Even hardside luggage today tends to have zippers, which always feels strange, as if things that do not belong together—the hardness of the suitcase, the softness of the zipper—have been joined. But when old, hardside suitcases like these Airways are open, the tops stay up, and you can drape things (a scarf, a T-shirt) over the edge, transforming them into mini-wardrobes that display your possessions. And when you close them, they feel closed.

Vintage luggage feels more closed than luggage today. One of the suitcases I have collected—a cream-colored marbled Samsonite from the mid-century "Fashiontone Luggage" line—has brass-colored clasps that click open and close and don't seem like they would be substantial at all, but then they bite down and don't budge. The suitcase is sturdy and feels like a case. When I open it, it lays flat, both sides the same depth, so there is no sense that there is a top or bottom apart from the orientation of the Samsonite key lock on the top, under the handle. The inside is lined with the kind of polyester that conjures silk. The fabric is a light khaki, almost a brown, and soft to the touch. On one side of the case are two ribbons that I can stretch across my clothes and run through a clasp. On the other side is a fabric panel that can be pulled over and then hooked on two hooks. The former owner plastered a red sticker on the top of the suitcase by the handle that reads, "LAURO LINES NAPLES," maybe from a cruise she took.

Most of my luggage was designed for women. Luggage design has tended to police the boundary between the masculine and the feminine, even today—let alone decades ago. Samsonite's designs from the middle of the last century make it abundantly clear that men are supposed to travel one way and women, another. One advertisement for the women's "Fashiontone" line notes the beauty and color of the pieces, as well as their relationship to the fashion industry: "Five lovely colors to go with the season's smartest travel clothes." (Sometimes this emphasis on fashion is more explicit—another 1950s ad that features a woman in a suit, holding a bouquet of flowers, reads: "Costume by Schiaparelli . . . Fashiontone Luggage by Samsonite.") The linings of the bags are "luxurious," and an open suitcase shows hats and high-heeled shoes arranged neatly. A customer might also purchase a matching "Hang-It-All" that "holds up to 8 dresses" in its "hang-up top" and "accessories, cosmetics and shoes" in the bottom.

Conversely, the word "man" appears with almost comic frequency in a Samsonite ad from the same period for a "Man-sized gift value" of "Man Tailored Luggage" in Admiral Blue, Natural Rawhide Finish, and Saddle Tan. The ad promises, "*Any* man will get a man-sized thrill out of this gift value! A matched set of *two* pieces of Samsonite for less than you'd expect to pay for just *one* piece of such fine quality luggage." The orgasmic "man-sized thrill" costs only $44.50 and involves a "Travel-Twosome" of a "Two-suiter" and "Quick-Tripper" in a "better-than-leather finish." One case is pictured open and lined with ties. The "Samsonite Man's Set" is "scientifically planned to carry everything a well-groomed man needs for an average trip . . . wrinkle-free!" Behind the image of the suitcases in the foreground, a middle-aged white man in a gray suit stands next to a Christmas tree, happily

FIGURE 4

reading his card. I actually have this suitcase in Saddle Tan. It is monogrammed J.A.B.

These advertisements remind us of "the power of convention in relation to gender and design in our society."[1]

Likewise, the "man bag" of the 1990s had to be designated as different from a purse in order to protect the carrier's masculinity; after all, one wouldn't want to be transformed into a woman. In a well-known episode of *Seinfeld*, Jerry finds himself uttering the cliché female line "I can never find anything in here" as he rummages through his "European carry-all." The other characters insist that the bag is a purse; Kramer calls him a "dandy" and a "fancy boy." When the bag is stolen, Jerry calls out to a police officer that he has been robbed and attempts to describe the bag (black, with a strap). The officer replies, "You mean a purse," and, exasperated and no longer defensive, Jerry finally agrees.[2]

Train cases are among the most traditionally feminine forms of luggage as they held cosmetics—and thus the key to beauty, as the ads would suggest. One of Samsonite's mid-century brands was called the "Ultralite Beauty Case." I have three train cases in my collection. One is light blue and monogrammed with the initials D.L.R. The inside is lined with pale blue plastic and smells like a clean Band-Aid. The former owner stuck a sticker of a cartoon raccoon to the lower right-hand corner of the mirror. The other case is from Amelia Earhart's luggage line, which capitalized on the aviatrix's fame during her lifetime and continued to be produced long after her death in 1937 by companies like American Tourister. Earhart had suggested to Samuel Orenstein of Newark's Orenstein Truck Company that travel by air required particular luggage designs; she then collaborated to design bent plywood cases with fabric covers.[3] My case is yellow with a strap across the top rather than a handle. The lock reads AMELIA EARHART. Earhart isn't the only icon to be immortalized in luggage. Luggage has played an integral role in celebrity culture, from Humphrey Bogart's "Bogie Bag" designed by Dupont in 1947 to Hermès's Kelly and Birkin bags—if we count purses as luggage—which embody different modes of iconic femininity: classic and ladylike (Grace Kelly) and artsy and bohemian (Jane Birkin).

I know a bit more about the former owner of the third train case, as her address tag is still attached: *Mrs. R.G. Weigand, 3921 Sterling St, Richmond, Va.* The "d" of "Weigand" and the "t" of "St" are hidden under the borders of the brown mock-leather tag. The letters have been typed on a typewriter, and the paper is yellowed with age. I looked up 3921 Sterling Street on Google Maps, and there it was: a bluish gray house with white trim and bushes out in front. A large tree in the front yard. A narrow concrete pathway up to the door. Mrs. R. G. Weigand probably doesn't live there anymore. Mrs. R. G. Weigand is probably dead. Richmond is a four-hour drive from me, and somehow this train case ended up in a vintage store in my city, away from its home. The case is not in great shape—it has a large splotch on the top, as if someone spilled nail polish remover or some other chemical on it—but it feels like it was used, like it was a part of someone's life. Although there was nothing in the case apart from the address tag when I bought it, I can imagine it filled with things: cosmetics and jewelry. Maybe letters and notes. The letters and notes of Mrs. R. G. Weigand. The inside smells waxy, like old lipstick.

You can't fill a train case with toiletries and carry it on an airplane today, but you can bring it with you in a car. And when you travel by car, you don't have to be an efficient packer. You can bring almost anything you like. Sometimes I pack my marbled Samsonite suitcase with books. Then it is really heavy. Sometimes I bring two or three of my vintage suitcases, packed with provisions both necessary and not. I have a light blue Starline case that looks like the one that Sharon McKendrick (Hayley Mills) carries to her tent at Camp Inch in *The Parent Trap* (1961). My sisters and I watched that movie again and again when we were younger. That might be why I bought the suitcase. On my long drives in the mountains of North Carolina and Tennessee, especially in the fall and spring, I see all the motorcyclists with their own, more space-conscious luggage: the rounded leather and canvas compartments on the back of their bikes that don't look like they would hold much at all, but they must.

My vintage luggage connects me to the past. I don't know what this past is, but I know it's there. These suitcases and train cases have stories to tell about unknown people and trips. Strangers and their strange movements around the globe. And now, the things these suitcases held are lost. Only the containers remain. But the luggage of today has memories and stories, too. The kind of remembering that suitcases give rise to is a peculiar kind of memory of things that are not quite forgotten, but not quite remembered either.

When I throw a suitcase up on my bed and unzip it, I think for a moment that I might find something in it—if not a thing (an old baggage claim ticket or a lost sock), then a sense of the past that comes with unzipping it yet again, for another trip. If I checked a bag the last time I took it somewhere, I always leave the tag on, so the next time I pull it out of the closet, there is a reminder of this last trip. Then I tear it off and throw it away.

When you aren't traveling, it's hard to know what to do with your luggage. It is inconvenient; it takes up space. If you live in a small apartment, you might store it under your bed. If you have a large suitcase and a small Rollaboard, you might zip the smaller one up in the larger one. Or you might store your winter or summer clothes in them, in which case they become almost a kind of furniture, like extra dresser drawers. When my sister Katharine lived in San Francisco, she stored her suitcases on a covered outdoor area off the kitchen of her old apartment because this was the only place the bags would fit. It was an odd place on the interior of the building—not a proper porch, but a nook that wasn't good for much else. Her bags and those of her boyfriend, now her husband, sat out there, semi-sheltered from the elements. We tend to keep our suitcases hidden away until we need them, so their visibility means travel. It means that we are going somewhere. My dog Millie knows this, and she paces around when I take out a suitcase, fearful that she will be left behind. I store my luggage—my normal, practical luggage, not my vintage luggage—in the closet in my bedroom, behind a row of hanging coats that brings to mind *The Lion, the Witch and the Wardrobe*. Here is the inventory:

Large suitcases:

Orange JUMP hardside suitcase
Light blue soft-sided Atlantic suitcase
Brown plaid London Fog suitcase

Carry-ons:

Light blue soft-sided Atlantic suitcase (matches the larger one)
Ricardo soft-sided suitcase (with fake Missoni-esque pattern)

Duffel bags:

LeSportsac bag (printed with the Eiffel Tower)
Orla Kiely for Target bag (printed with cars)
Black pleather bag
Small bag printed with the design of grass (from Decathlon in Paris)
Three very large, rolling black bags

I use it all, apart from the London Fog suitcase. This one is quite large, and I worry that I would be tempted to fill it up, and then—if I'm flying somewhere—I would find myself hit with enormous overweight baggage charges. But the company's film-noir advertisements suggest that my suitcase and I are destined to end up on a cobblestone street, under a streetlamp, in the fog. In this scenario, I will no doubt be dressed in a trench coat. The Atlantic suitcases are sort of ugly; they were on sale. But I like my orange JUMP suitcase. I have a habit of acquiring things when I travel, so I have been known to need another bag to bring these acquisitions home. This is how I obtained this orange suitcase in Paris several years ago: I bought it at Les Galleries Lafayette because I had bought too many books and couldn't get them all home in my small suitcase. I hadn't seen the brand before, but I liked the look of it, and I liked the lining, which is printed with the phrase "For the happy few since 1979," which I take to be a reference to the king's famous St. Crispin's Day speech in Shakespeare's *Henry V*. After picking it out, I wheeled it to a café in the store where I could look out over everything— the cupola above, the cosmetics displays below, and the mannequins everywhere—and I sat and had a glass of wine and surveyed the glittering palace of stained glass and gold.

It feels a bit indulgent to buy luggage while on a trip, but I justified it by telling myself that it would probably be more expensive to mail the things home. And overweight baggage fees are steep. Years ago, when I was flying out of Heathrow, I realized that my bag was too heavy. The fee was enormous, and I think I must have looked slightly panicked, because a kind and efficient Virgin Atlantic employee came to my rescue, instructing me to open the bag and figure out what I could carry. She surveyed the contents and started pulling out clothing and books. "You're going to need to carry these books," she said. "And this—put on these boots. These are heavy. Put those shoes you're wearing back in here." She continued to rummage around. "Put this coat on over your jacket. And wrap this scarf around you." She got the bag down to the proper weight and saved me the fee. I'm heartened that Jane Austen had a tendency to acquire things in her travels, as well. In a letter to Cassandra from June 2, 1799, she writes that "I am afraid I cannot undertake to carry Martha's Shoes home, for tho' we had plenty of room in our Trunks when we came, We shall have many more things to take back, & I must allow besides for my packing."[4] She doesn't seem to think much of her packing. She acknowledges that she might be able to fit more in the trunk if she arranged her possessions differently, but I like her resistance to the idea of being a good packer, as well as the intimacy that the phrase implies: Cassandra is clearly no stranger to Jane's subpar packing skills. *My packing.* You understand.

When I left New York City, where I had lived for most of my adult life, to take a job at my college in North Carolina, I checked two huge black duffel bags with me on the flight. (Not the same ones I have now; I gave these two away years ago.) I paid the airline's fee for extra and overweight baggage as it seemed easier than shipping things. One of the bags held an air mattress, which I slept on the first night in my new, empty apartment. That morning, I had deflated the mattress after my last night in my old apartment, stamping on it to get out all the air, then folding it up and packing it away. I slid the bags down four flights of stairs and loaded them into a cab bound for LaGuardia. Several days earlier, my friend Jon and I had put my sofa out on the street. It was my last piece of furniture, and I had been unable to sell it on Craigslist. We figured that if we put it out, someone would come and take it away, but almost immediately after we left it, it started to rain—a real summer tempest—and the sofa was ruined. Before I got into the cab, I looked at the soaking wet last remnant of my apartment. Everything else was in the duffel bags. But I still go back to the city some summers, and then, I fill my three large black duffel bags with clothes, books, dishes, bed linens, towels, books, even my laser printer—everything I need for the small room I have rented at General Theological Seminary. I don't know how I got the bags up the stairs. I bought them at the end of one summer, at one of the luggage stores in Times Square that smell of chemicals. The men who worked at the store brought the bags up from storage, packed flat and wrapped in plastic.

When I was younger, a trip to the luggage department of a department store was a ritual, the first step of a trip. I looked at all the different colors and sizes of bags, the matching sets arranged on small platforms like actors on a stage, each one suggesting a different kind of trip. In *Say Anything* (1989), Diane's father John Court (John Mahoney) goes to a luggage department to buy his daughter a present for her trip to Europe, and his credit card is declined. This is the first step in the revelation of his criminal activities and the unraveling of his life. The scene is humiliating, in part because he had been flirting with the saleslady. He leaves the store empty-handed. *Joe Versus the Volcano* (1990) depicts a more comic shopping trip. The salesman (Barry McGovern) assures Joe (Tom Hanks) that luggage is the "central preoccupation of my life" and reminds him, "You travel the world, you're away from home—perhaps away from your family. All you have to depend on is yourself. And your luggage." Joe's description of his journey to the Pacific island Waponi Woo poses a "luggage problem" that the salesman solves by presenting Joe with a watertight steamer trunk that he rolls out of a small chapel-like room. Joe buys four and, ultimately, he will have to fasten them together as a raft to survive: he *really* depends on them. Now many people order their luggage online or buy it from specialty luggage stores. Luggage departments still exist, but their day has passed. Suitcases have become less expensive over the last couple of decades, but also, in some cases, cheaper in construction. Now, a suitcase might last a couple of years before a wheel breaks off or the zipper busts. But these bags in the past lasted. The choice you made was an important one because you would live with it for some time. There was also something thrilling about leaving the department store with a suitcase. It was still empty. It had its tags. It had not yet become what it would become. It was all promise. And if you happened to be shopping for other things when you bought your suitcase, you could store them away in it.

Luggage was a popular high school graduation gift, particularly matched luggage. It was a middle-class symbol of adulthood: you were leaving home. My classmates probably already had enough luggage to get them to college, but proper college luggage needed to match, and it needed to be purchased *because* you were going to college. When I went to college in New York in 1995, I did not take matched luggage with me. Instead, I checked two big, black duffel bags (these things seem to define my life), and one of them might have been the same duffel bag that accompanied me to summer camp when I was younger. The camp was on a ranch in the mountains of northern California, up a long and winding highway. I remember dragging the bag through the dust and into the bunkhouse, where I shoved it under my bed. I had to kick it a few times to get it tucked away. There was enough room under each bunk for two large bags: yours and your bunkmate's. These duffels were amorphous blobs, seemingly expanding in all directions. Mine smelled like plastic, and it held all of the required camp things: a flashlight, bug spray, and clothing marked with my name on iron-on tags. Its underside was always covered in dust and dirt.

When I was in college, and for a number of years after college, I had a large Eagle Creek backpack. It was dark green and black, and I took it to Turkey, France, and other places. I dumped it on the floor of many hostels. This was how I traveled and how my friends traveled then. We never brought suitcases. But you could lay the backpack flat and unzip it like a suitcase. This was a popular design, and more than one person advised me: *Don't buy a top-loading backpack. You'll never be able to get to anything.* These were also the days of "money belts," as we called them: envelope-like polyester security pouches that you wore around your waist, the strap adjusted for snugness. These zippered pouches were generally for international travel. They held your passport, traveler's checks, and cash (you always withdrew some cash before setting off and stored photocopies of your passport in your backpack). And you wore the belt on the plane and then all the time, wherever you were. Late in the days on hot summer days, the belt became very sweaty against your stomach, under or just above the waist of your jeans, and you could always sort of see it—a faint bulge—and feel it, especially when you sat down. The money belt was the distillation of all travel anxiety: the sense that you were vulnerable once you left home, that thieves were everywhere. To carry a purse was madness—it will be snatched. A daypack?—Lunacy. Someone will get into it when you're in a crowd. This is what you were told. But the ugly yellowish-cream–colored money belt promised to protect you.

Luggage is not always about the practical. My parents had a matching set of Hartmann tan tweed luggage when I was growing up: two suitcases, one larger than the other, with combination locks. They had tiny little wheels that didn't actually roll and short straps that could be attached, but if you actually tried to pull the suitcases, they fell over. My dad thought they might have been a gift from his father because he had too much luggage and wanted to get rid of some of it. We called him "Poppy." Or that his wife Jeanie, our grandmother, might have bought them for him. When she was younger, Jeanie was a professional shopper for I. Magnin & Company, a department store that doesn't exist anymore. My grandfather was an executive at Weinstock's, another department store that doesn't exist anymore, and this is how they met. Jeanie helped stylish, wealthy women build their wardrobes. She was also a collector—an amazing collector with collections that filled their house. But my mom remembers buying the suitcases at Weinstock's in Sacramento. She wanted them desperately, and she waited for them to go on sale. My parents took this luggage to Paris, Hawaii, San Francisco, other places. The suitcases had brass hardware and were trimmed in tan leather and lined in toile, and there was a fabric patch inside where you could write your name and address, a detail that seems oddly personal given that, if the bags were lost, surely luggage tags on the outside of the bag would be consulted. The suitcases were heavy, even when empty. Now, this heft would be considered a design flaw, and my parents haven't traveled with these bags for years. But decades ago, these behemoth bags were heavy because they were supposed to be heavy. This was part of the peculiar character of these objects. Their weight made them weighty—substantial—like the feeling of going somewhere.

Our grandparents may not have given my parents this Hartmann luggage, but they did give me and my sisters suitcases for Christmas one year. I don't think the suitcases rolled, but they were small, and they were all the same bag in different colors: navy blue, forest green, and black. Mine was the green one. They were soft-sided, and each had a band of stripes across them. We took these bags when we visited them in Phoenix, and on these visits they took us to see mesas and botanical gardens of cacti, and we ate prickly pear jelly, which we brought back with us in the suitcases. I don't know what happened to these bags. My parents still have the old Hartmann suitcases. And it's easy to find them on eBay. I came across one set that was listed as "Vintage Hartmann Belting Leather and Tweed Suitcases," with this description: "I have four Vintage Hartmann bags listed and all are beautiful. I bought them with the intent of traveling with them. All but one has been displayed in my office as works of art and nostalgia. That said, these were made for the road, and probably belong there."

Works of art. Emblems of memory. Things that should be on the road.

The weather has caused a number of flights to be cancelled, and lots of people don't make it to the conference. Some of the papers at the big paper sessions have to be read by other people. I'm still enjoying the hotel, although I stand toward the inside of the elevator as I go up. At night, I walk out on my balcony. There isn't any furniture out there, so I just stand and look out over the city and think about nothing.

The conference side of my suitcase is filling up with dirty clothes. After I wear something, I fold it up and put it back in the suitcase. I can map out the days in folded clothes. In the morning, I order room service (Eggs Benedict and coffee) and look over at the other queen bed in the room, and the clothes spread out on it, and wonder what I should wear.

I meet a friend for lunch after the morning panel, and then we go shopping for bourbon. She lives close to me, in Greensboro, and we both like bourbon. But North Carolina's state-run liquor stores have a pretty limited selection, particularly when it comes to something out of the ordinary. She picks out two nice bottles and then hands them off to me. She's flying, so she can't take them with her, but I can drive them home. Back in my room, I wrap the bottles up in my worn clothes and tuck in into my suitcase.

The conference ends the next day. It appears that in a slightly drunken state the night before, I dropped one of my contact lenses on the bathroom counter instead of into the case, and it dried up. I don't have another pair, so I put on my glasses for the drive home. I pack my suitcase and load it into my car and pick Millie up and head for the North Carolina mountains.

I have decided to stay in a small town called Brevard for the night. The area is known for its waterfalls.

We drive through Nantahala National Forest, and the trees are quiet and the sun is low. I pull over at scenic overlooks. We pass through a horrible rich town called Highlands that is all country clubs and golf courses. It's Sunday, so everything is closed and no one is around. I find a Wendy's and stop for a mid-afternoon cheeseburger snack. Wendy's isn't high on my fast-food list. When I drive through the Southeast, I look for Five Guys first, then Cook Out, then Dairy Queen, then Sonic, then Wendy's. That is my ranking of road trip cheeseburgers, not taking into account options available in other parts of the country, like In-N-Out, Whataburger, and Braum's.

In the late afternoon, we drive up to a retro place called the Sunset Motel, where pink flamingos welcome us. I am tired from socializing and glad to be alone. While I take a shower, Millie sits on the bath mat and watches the door, as she always does. My suitcase sits on one of the queen beds, watching over us, too.

5 LOST LUGGAGE: ALABAMA'S UNCLAIMED BAGGAGE CENTER

I pull into the parking lot of the Unclaimed Baggage Center on a gray afternoon entirely suited to a temple of lost things. Lost things come to Scottsboro, Alabama. Well, not all lost things, but lost things in lost luggage.

But I am not lost. I have driven through mountains and past fireworks megastores (each one is always the last and biggest one) and dead dogs rotting on the side of the road, to reckon with one of Alabama's top tourist attractions. The center looks like a standard office park, apart from the blue and orange UNCLAIMED BAGGAGE CENTER sign shaped like a suitcase. I had some trouble finding the place, so I stopped in front of a huge church to look up directions. Willow Street is a little way off the highway, past a Budget Inn, a Family Dollar, some muffler places, lumber companies, and

FIGURE 5

pawn shops, and the Scottsboro Boys Museum and Cultural Center. The building is lined by neatly trimmed hedges, and two American flags frame the entrance. A glider, several rocking chairs, and hanging planters suggest the front porch of a house rather than a business.

Without our luggage, we're set loose in the world unprepared. This is the anxiety at the heart of lost luggage. When I traveled to Montreal several years ago, my suitcase didn't arrive. It is a strange feeling to walk out of an airport without a bag. Passing under signs in French, I felt more than empty-handed: I felt dangerously light, as if I didn't belong where I was. The next day, I went shopping and bought a black sweater and black slacks—I might have been in mourning for my suitcase, which was delivered to my hotel the next day. In *On Beauty and Being Just*, Elaine Scarry understands the recognition of beauty in relationship to late luggage:

> A beautiful object is suddenly present, not because a new object has entered the sensory horizon bringing its beauty with it (as when a new poem is written or a new student arrives or a willow tree, unleafed by winter, becomes electric—a maze of yellow wands lifting against lavender clapboards and skies) but because an object, already within the horizon has its beauty, like late luggage, suddenly placed in your hands.[1]

Apprehending the beauty of a new thing is sudden, as is its already-there-presence. When you lose your bag, you fear you will never see it again, and then, suddenly, you do. We take for granted that we get to keep our luggage with us when we travel today. It may be taken away from us for periods of time, but it does not generally travel separately from us, as in the past. In this sense, the transport of luggage used to resemble mailing a package. And like a package, trunks were banged about a bit, sometimes causing their contents to be damaged. In her letters to Cassandra, Jane Austen writes of her woes with her trunk. In a letter from May 17, 1799, she writes of the problem of its weight:

I have some hopes of being plagued about my Trunk;—I *had* more a few hours ago, for it was too heavy to go by the Coach which brought Thomas & Rebecca from Devizes, there was reason to suppose that it might be too heavy likewise for any other Coach, & for a long time we could hear of no Waggon to convey it.—At last however, we unluckily discovered that one was just on the point of setting out for this place—but at any rate, the Trunk cannot be here till tomorrow—so far we are safe—& who knows what may not happen to procure a farther delay.[2]

In another letter dated June 15 to 17, 1808, one of the "important nothings" she communicates again concerns her trunk: "Would you believe it my trunk is come already; and, what completes the wondrous happiness, nothing is damaged."[3] The humorous hyperbole of "wondrous happiness" is classic Austen, but it also hints at the frequency with which trunks might be delayed or their contents harmed. It *is* wondrous that her possessions are not damaged, and she is relieved. And in her news to Cassandra from March 2 to 3, 1814, she is not so lucky: "My Trunk did not come last night, I suppose it will this morning; if not I must borrow Stockings & buy Shoes & Gloves for my visit. I was foolish not to provide better against such a Possibility. I have great hope however that writing about it in this way, will bring the Trunk presently."[4] Here, she jokes that she might conjure the trunk into existence by writing, thus remedying the problem of her self-proclaimed foolishness. This is a foolishness we all feel at some point in traveling.

Austen got her things back. She was lucky. The Unclaimed Baggage Center is a place of unrecovered things, and shoppers come in search of these ownerless things. The 40,000 square-foot center opened in 1970 and draws over 800,000 visitors per year from over 40 countries. Its status as a major attraction is underscored by a display of tourist brochures at the entrance for local vineyards, zoos, skydiving, golfing, caverns, state parks, and the North Alabama Hallelujah Trail of Sacred Places. You can also buy souvenir T-shirts. The departments in the main store include jewelry, sporting goods, formalwear, books, electronics ("Purchase Limit 3 Laptops Per Guest Per Day"), men's and women's clothing, and (of course) luggage. There is a Starbucks. A separate building—the "Etc." store—houses children's items and housewares. The parking lot is about halfway full, and several campers testify to the store's status as a vacation destination. A sign off to the side of the building indicates that there is more RV parking out back. There is nothing distinctive about the location. Next door is Alabama Tires and a Citgo. Across the street is a T and W Unclaimed Baggage, which looks rather run-down in comparison with Unclaimed Baggage. (One Unclaimed Baggage employee describes it as "a knock-off.") Behind the center is a cemetery: Cedar Hill Cemetery, where, according to their website, twenty of the city's 63 acres are available at $400 per grave or a four-grave plot for $1,400. There are graves from the Civil War. And the graves of some of the city's first families. And dogwood trees.

The center receives bags from airlines, bus lines, trains, cruise ships, rental car companies, and resorts. The center also sells unclaimed cargo. Airline travel accounts for the majority of unclaimed luggage. According to the Unclaimed Baggage Center's website, 99.5 percent of bags are picked up at baggage claim. But then there is the other 0.5 percent. In 2012, over 1.8 million bags were lost, stolen or damaged by major US airlines on domestic flights. This means that slightly over three bags were mishandled per 1,000 passengers, an 8 percent decline since the year before. In 2007, the situation was far worse: 4.5 million bags were lost or damaged.[5] In 2013, the number of mishandled bags worldwide was 21.8 million, or 6.96 bags per 1,000 passengers.[6] Regional and budget airlines tend to have the worst track records. Radio frequency microchips such as SuperSmart Tag and Rebound Tag promise travelers that what is lost will indeed be found, but such devices only serve as reminders of the unpredictability of travel. According to the website of the Unclaimed Baggage Center, airlines conduct "an extensive three-month tracing process" to try to find the unclaimed bags' owners, and claims are paid on the remaining lost bags. Then they sell the "unclaimed baggage property"—now no longer the property of anyone—to the center.

The center's website is at pains to note that the process of trying to find the bags' owners is a thorough one and results in "an astonishingly small fraction of a percent of bags that are ultimately orphaned." *Orphaned.* The word suggests that a bag's owner is its parent, and this parent has died. The website uses the terms "lost" and "unclaimed" interchangeably. "Lost" implies that the bag was misplaced, as you might lose your keys, but also that its movements have become untraceable. "Unclaimed" implies that it has been abandoned. This abandonment is related to its status as lost, but its status as lost can't entirely account for it. These orphaned bags are bought sight-unseen and arrive by the tractor-trailer load at the center's processing facility, where they are opened, sorted, and priced. Over 7,000 new items arrive everyday. Clothing is laundered or dry cleaned at an in-house facility that is the largest in northern Alabama. Electronics are tested and wiped of personal data. Fine jewelry is cleaned and appraised. Bags are opened at 2:30 p.m. on Mondays through Saturdays for the public, so you can peer into a stranger's suitcase before everything is removed. The staff sorts out "the best items" for retail, and approximately half of the remaining items are donated through their Reclaimed for Good program. The other half, which are "unsuitable for retail or donation," are thrown away. This process is represented on the website by an image of an open suitcase; its contents are divided into the three categories of SELL, DONATE, and TRASH lower down on the page. The category of "trash" includes a pacifier, a Sharpie, paper clips, a rubber band, a tube of toothpaste and a toothbrush, a small brown Field Notes notebook, and a folded piece of paper that appears to be a receipt or a page that has been torn out of a book. That one-quarter of this lost property is worthless strikes me as outrageously sad. You can't do much with someone's toothpaste and toothbrush. Or with her notebook. The valueless objects that fill our bags and make up our lives.

But these bags also contain odd and extraordinary things. The entrance to the center is designated as a "museum" of found objects and presided over by a portrait of founders Doyle and Sue Owens. Sue is seated in a yellow armchair and Doyle stands above her, with his hand on her shoulder. To the right is a display of "Religious Objects," and to the left is the puppet goblin Hoggle from the 1986 film *Labyrinth*, who arrived at the center in 1997 in "deteriorating condition" and was restored. These displays continue in the store itself, where treasures are mounted high on the walls, including moose antlers, Underwood typewriters, and musical instruments, including a Russian Domra and an Afghan Rubab. These objects are accompanied by signs that identify and describe them ("Afghans have a special feeling for the rubab") and indicate when they arrived at the center. A "Handmade Ship Model, HMS Surprise" includes a brief history lesson on the Napoleonic Wars and a picture of Russell Crowe in the film *Master and Commander*. An "Antique Flirting Fan" from 2010 is assigned a story: "This beautifully hand painted fan from the 1800's shows classical scenes of youths at their leisure. Gilded in gold with intricately carved bone sticks, this Victorian fan must have belonged to a lady of significant social standing." These objects are not for sale, and some

FIGURE 6

displays throughout the store feature items that are not for sale, including several vintage suitcases.

I stand by the rows of pale gray shopping carts and look at my map. Rows of jeans stretch out in front of me, folded in half and hung on clip hangers. I walk through the section for uniforms, past of a vat of lace-trimmed leg warmers (a shopper has abandoned a motel-room-style black pleather Holy Bible among these garments), and into the formalwear room, which is filled with long, brightly-colored dresses that bring to mind prom in the 1990s. Mass-produced wedding dresses—David's Bridal sort of stuff—are hung six or so dresses deep against the wall: all sequins, lace, and taffeta. I wonder if they have been worn. I wander past racks of button-up shirts, robes, and pajamas. Some of the store's most expensive items—an ivory lace Chloé dress, size 12 ($849.99; Retails $3,195.00) and a "Sherazade Trunk" by the Barrel Shack ($189.99; Retails: $1,450.00)—are singled out and arranged on top of the racks, set apart from a sea of everyday things as reminders of the treasures lurking in lost bags. One woman looks up at the Chloé dress.

"How could someone not claim a Chloé dress?" she asks her friend, shaking her head. "Amazing."

The vast majority of items are ordinary. Costume jewelry. Blouses, dresses, T-shirts. Rows of point-and-shoot cameras and mass-market paperbacks. The things of everyday life. But the tension between the ordinary and the extraordinary— not far from the café is an intricately carved dark wood frame labeled "Nineteenth-Century Swiss Black Forest $1350.00"— gives the center its character. In fine jewelry, the cases are filled with bangle bracelets, watches, pearl necklaces, cameo brooches and pendants, gold crosses encrusted with diamonds, and gold and silver chains of all lengths. I survey the price tags, which are strangely precise: $103.99, $66.99, $172.99, $260.99, $500.99.

A man next to me asks the saleswoman if he can see a cameo ring, and she takes it out of the case and hands it to him.

FIGURE 7

"This one is really pretty," she says. "We had another one like this that was a real bargain. It got snapped up."

He looks at it carefully and turns it over. "Yes, that's real nice."

"It's a beauty. And there's this other one with the pearl, which has a really unique setting."

She hands him the other ring, which he slips on the end of his finger, as far as it will go, as if contemplating what it would look like on a woman's hand.

"Hmm," he says. "This one is a find."

I walk over to the scarf section. Another saleswoman notices my ring—a skull—and smiles.

"Do you like skulls?" she asks.

"I do," I say.

"Well, I have something to show you that just came in." She walks away for a moment and returns holding a neatly folded black-and-white skull scarf.

"Alexander McQueen," she says.

"Ooh. That's lovely."

"It just came in."

"Wow," I say. "There are some beautiful things here, too," I say, gesturing at the scarves in the case.

"Yes," she says. "Hermès."

One of the scarves is a deep blue. "Can I see that one?" I ask. She takes it out and places it on the counter.

"We also have this one," she says, pointing to another one. "Really gorgeous."

"I think that's a little too classic for me," I say. "Horses and what-not."

She laughs. "Yes, for me, too," she says. "But this blue one is beautiful." It is. I unfold it on the counter. The pattern is an angel.

I think of the suitcase that held this scarf. Maybe it was locked. Or maybe it wasn't. Maybe it doesn't matter. Suitcase locks have never struck me as a legitimate form of security. Perhaps it is their size: little metal things with a keyhole or combination locks with tiny buttons. They bring to mind the lock on your diary when you're a kid: more symbolic than anything, about proclaiming that something should not be opened rather than that it can't be. An assertion of privacy, not a protection of it. And now the scarf is here, orphaned. I decide to buy it, and the saleswoman smiles approvingly.

"I'll have it for you at the register when you're ready," she says. "No rush."

"Thanks," I say. "I can go ahead and pay."

I hand her my debit card, and she swipes it: $129.99. $141.69 with tax. The scarf is a splurge, but I don't regret it. Now its value is determined by the market, not by sentiment or memory. When this scarf was taken out of its suitcase, its connection to its owner was lost. The suitcases that enclose these things also define them, and the things mean less, or differently, apart from them.

Before I leave, I walk out behind the building to the cemetery and stand under the iron archway, watching people come and go from their cars, their shopping bags in hand. The unanswered question of the Unclaimed Baggage Center is why the bags remain unclaimed. When I told people I was coming here, that is what they always asked: *Why wouldn't you claim your bag?* Perhaps there is no answer to this question. Or the answer is that it is unanswered, unanswerable. The things at vintage stores or antiques malls have been brought there—sold or donated—or the stores' owners have acquired them somewhere. Maybe the objects' former owners died. Maybe their former owners moved and were getting rid of things. But Unclaimed Baggage is different. Perhaps it is not that the objects are lost, but that their owners are. These people hover over the center like ghosts, and no one knows what to say about them.

My scarf is folded in a white paper bag, the top stapled shut with the receipt. I take it out. It is soft. It doesn't feel new; it feels like something that belonged to someone. I hold it up and look at it. The angel's expression is inscrutable, almost childlike, her green wings resting behind her, her head crowned with flowers. She wears a cape that is parted and falls at her sides, but she doesn't really have sides as she has no body. Inside the cape, in place of a torso, is a void. Nothing. Only a geometric pattern like broken glass. She flaps in the breeze, and I think she is the angel of unclaimed bags, taking everything into her nothingness.

I tie the scarf around my head to keep my hair out of my eyes while I drive home.

I sleep as you can only sleep after three days at a Shakespeare conference. Today: waterfalls. I make coffee and take Millie for a morning walk along the residential streets. I like the motel's old sign. It isn't cloyingly nostalgic; it has just been there for a while.

When I check out, the woman in the front office recommends a café down the street for breakfast.

"It's just in a strip mall across from the college," she says. "But it's good."

There, I order a breakfast burrito and more coffee to go and then drive down the town's main street for several miles, toward the entrance to Pisgah National Forest. There aren't many other cars in the park, maybe because it's Monday. At Looking Glass Falls, we stand by the side of the road and watch the water. A mosquito gets me on the finger. At Sliding Rock, we wait to see if anyone will come sliding down, but it's not open for the season yet. I eat my breakfast burrito at a picnic bench by the river and drink my coffee from the Styrofoam cup and listen to the water. On the way out of the park, I stop at the gift shop and buy souvenirs for myself and for friends. The gift shop is watched over by a taxidermy bear that resembles Smokey Bear.

Then, home. I always unpack right away. Unpacking feels like putting a house back together, as if you have taken things away from it and need to replace them for it to be whole again. I drag my suitcase upstairs to my bedroom and open it on the bed and set to work. The books go back on my stacks of books or out on the front porch. Most of the clothes are dirty and go in the hamper. A suitcase at the end of a trip is a suitcase filled with laundry.

The souvenirs are still wrapped up in my clothes, so I unwrap them and line them up on my comforter. Here is the inventory: snow globe from Helen (depicting not the town, but a Disney-esque castle), two porcelain wooden shoe miniatures and six magnets, also from Helen; a small, pink North Carolina piggy bank from a gas station; a Sliding Rock mug; five Smokey Bear magnets; two Smokey Bear patches; three Smokey Bear pins (one of which I pinned to the sun visor in my car); and a Pisgah National Forest sticker, which I stick to my suitcase. I take the souvenirs and my friend's bourbon downstairs and set the bourbon on the kitchen counter and send her an e-mail to see when she'd like to come pick it up. I keep two of the Helen magnets and one of the Smokey magnets and put them on my fridge, squeezing them in among my collection.

Then I go back upstairs and put my suitcase in the closet, way in the back.

ACKNOWLEDGMENTS

Thank you to Christopher Schaberg, Ian Bogost, and Haaris Naqvi for including me in this wonderful series and for their thoughtful edits and feedback. I am also grateful to the design team for the beautiful cover, to Katherine De Chant and Laura Ewen in marketing, and to Leela Ulaganathan and James Tupper in production. Thanks are also due to Michelle Tessler and to my agent Jim McCarthy and everyone at Dystel, Goderich & Bourret. I am grateful, always, to John Archer for his unfailing support of my academic and non-academic writing. I was fortunate to have had the combined brain power of the members of the Materiality and Modernity seminar at Wake Forest University: Candace Mixon, Claudia Kairoff, Jessica Richard, Laura Veneskey, Megan Mulder, Monique O'Connell, Morna O'Neill and Stephanie Koscak. Wanda Balzano and Paige Meltzer kindly invited me to talk about my work at the Women's Gender and Sexuality Studies Colloquium. I would also like to thank Wake Forest University for a research grant that allowed me to work at the collections of the New-York Historical Society, where Alexandra Krueger and Jill

Reichenbach were extremely helpful. I also thoroughly enjoyed my days in the newly restored Rose Reading Room at the New York Public Library, as well as in the Allen Room, thanks to Melanie Locay. Thank you to the Dunedin Public Art Gallery for allowing me to reproduce Jacques Joseph Tissot's *Waiting for a Train (Willesden Junction)* and to the Metropolitan Museum of Art for *Habit de Mallettier Coffrettier*. In the process of writing this book, I found that virtually everyone has something to say about luggage: a story or memory about a suitcase, a thought about a film or a book, a packing methodology. So thank you to everyone who shared these things with me or chatted with me about the project, including Audra Abt, Laura Aull, Elizabeth Bearden, Rian Bowie, Anne Boyle, Jane Carr, Amy Catanzano, Erin Chapman, Allison Devers, Lara Dodds, Michelle Dowd, Irina Dumitrescu, Meredith Farmer, Jon Farina, Jen Feather, Dean Franco, Sharon Fulton, Laura Giovanelli, Manda Goltz, Jennifer Greiman, Omaar Hena, Sarah Hogan, Jeff Holdridge, Melissa Jenkins, Kristina Kaufman, Catherine Keyser, Alison Kinney, Sara Landreth, Sarah Landreth, Cristina Marcelo, Sam Meyer, Patrick Moran, Anne Moyer, Francie Neukom, Kelly Neukom, Niamh O'Leary, Adrienne Pilon, Dan Quiles, Jenny Raab, Emily Richard, Anne Boyd Rioux, Joanna Ruocco, Randi Soloman, Jen Spitzer, Kelly Stage, Cassie Thomas, Olga Valbuena, Ania Wajnberg, Lauren Walsh, and Jessica Wolfe. Particular thanks are due to Jo Scutts, Sarah Torretta Klock, Erika Jaeggli, and Amanda Thompson for their excellent company as road-tripping buddies and to Jenny Pyke, Carter Smith, and Eric Ekstrand for long talks about books at home on my porch. Home is also vastly improved by Morna O'Neill and Jay Curley, who are wonderful in all ways. And to Ms. Fels and Ms. LaMay—your teachers when you're young are often the most important. My parents Brad and Sharon and my siblings Derek, Katharine, and Helen have also offered a tremendous amount of support. Thank you to the Riverstone Lodge in Townsend, Tennessee, for being the greatest motel ever; I wrote a lot of this there and on the road. And I don't think I could write a word without my dog Millie. She is my constant writing and traveling companion.

LIST OF ILLUSTRATIONS

NOTES

Introduction

1 Rebecca West, *Black Lamb and Grey Falcon: A Journey Through Yugoslavia* (New York: Penguin, 2007), 29.

2 Lori Brister, "Tourism in the Age of Mechanical Reproduction: Aesthetics and Advertisements in Travel Posters and Luggage Labels," in *Britain and the Narration of Travel in the Nineteenth Century: Texts, Images, Objects*, ed. Kate Hill (Burlington, VT: Ashgate, 2016), 130–49, 130.

3 Sam Todd, "Oh, the Places This Bag Has Been," *New York Times*, June 11, 2017, Styles section, 3.

4 Paul Fussell, *Abroad: British Literary Traveling Between the Wars* (Oxford and New York: Oxford University Press, 1980), 167.

5 See Homer, *The Odyssey*, ed. Alan Mandelbaum (New York: Bantam, 1990).

6 Eric J. Leed, *Mind of the Traveler: From Gilgamesh to Global Tourism* (New York: Basic Books, 1991), 27.

7 Miguel de Cervantes, *Don Quixote*, tr. Edith Grossman (New York: Harper Perennial, 2005), 5.

8 Cervantes, *Don Quixote*, 27.

9 Eric G. E. Zuelow, *A History of Modern Tourism* (New York: Palgrave Macmillan, 2016), 5–6.

10 Zuelow, *A History of Modern Tourism*, 7.

11 J. G. Links, "Notes on Foreign Travel," in *Bon Voyage: Designs for Travel*, Deborah Sampson Shinn, J. G. Links, et al. (New York: Cooper-Hewitt Museum, 1986), 17–53, 19.

12 Links, "Notes on Foreign Travel," 24.

13 Ibid., 53.

14 Zuelow, *A History of Modern Tourism*, 8.

15 Leed, "Notes on Foreign Travel," 11.

16 Cindy S. Aron, *Working at Play: A History of Vacations in the United States* (Oxford: Oxford University Press, 1999), 32.

17 Zuelow, *A History of Modern Tourism*, 1.

18 Links, "Notes on Foreign Travel," 30–31.

19 Paul Fussell, "Bourgeois Travel: Techniques and Artifacts," in *Bon Voyage: Designs for Travel*, Deborah Sampson Shinn, J. G. Links, et al. (New York: Cooper-Hewitt Museum, 1986), 55–93, 55.

20 Links, "Notes on Foreign Travel," 29.

21 Fussell, "Bourgeois Travel: Techniques and Artifacts," 55–56.

22 Ibid., 56.

23 Ibid., 58.

24 Ibid., 56–57, 67.

25 Ibid., 78.

26 Kristoffer A. Garin, *Devils on the Deep Blue Sea: The Dreams, Schemes, and Showdowns That Built America's Cruise-Ship Empires* (New York: Viking, 2005), 8.

27 Garin, *Devils on the Deep Blue Sea*, 13.

28 Ibid., 14.

29 Ibid.

30 Garin, *Devils on the Deep Blue Sea*, 15.

31 Fussell, "Bourgeois Travel: Techniques and Artifacts," 61.

32 Ibid., 73.

33 Ibid., 93.

34 Erin Blakemore, "Five Things To Know About Pullman Porters," Smithsonian.com, June 30, 2016, https://www.smithsonianmag.com/smart-news/five-things-know-about-pullman-porters-180959663/

35 All material from Marguerite S. Shaffer, "Seeing the Nature of America: The National Parks as National Assets, 1914–1929," in *Being Elsewhere: Tourism, Consumer Culture, and Identity in Modern Europe and North America*, ed. Shelley Baranowski and Ellen Furlough (Ann Arbor: University of Michigan Press, 2001), 155–84, 155.

36 Michael Berkowitz, "A 'New Deal' for Leisure: Making Mass Tourism during the Great Depression," in *Being Elsewhere: Tourism, Consumer Culture, and Identity in Modern Europe and North America*, ed. Shelley Baranowski and Ellen Furlough (Ann Arbor: University of Michigan Press, 2001), 185–212, 185 and 188.

37 Anthony Sampson, *Empires of the Sky: The Politics, Contests and Cartels of World Airlines* (New York: Random House, 1984), 43.

38 Sampson, *Empires of the Sky*, 36.

39 Patrick Smith, *Cockpit Confidential: Everything You Need to Know About Air Travel* (Chicago: Sourcebooks, 2013), xv.

40 Elizabeth Becker, *Overbooked: The Exploding Business of Travel and Tourism* (New York: Simon & Schuster, 2013), 9.

41 Becker, *Overbooked: The Exploding Business of Travel and Tourism*, 11, 12.

42 Ibid., 11.

43 Dean MacCannell, *The Tourist: A New Theory of the Leisure Class* (Berkeley and Los Angeles: University of California Press, 1999), 42.

44 Fussell, "Bourgeois Travel: Techniques and Artifacts," 65.

45 Daniel A. Gross, "The History of the Humble Suitcase," Smithsonian.com, May 9, 2014, https://www.smithsonianmag.com/history/history-humble-suitcase-180951376/

46 Joe Sharkey, "Reinventing the Suitcase by Adding the Wheel," *New York Times*, October 4, 2010, http://www.nytimes.com/2010/10/05/business/05road.html.

47 Ibid.

48 Stirling Kelso, Jennifer Coogan, Nina Fedrizzi, Emily Hsieh, Alison Miller, and Nicholas Teddy, "History of Airline Bags," *Travel+Leisure*, August 11, 2010, http://www.travelandleisure.com/articles/history-of-airline-baggage.

49 Smith, *Cockpit Confidential*, 265–66.

50 Ibid., 13.

51 Ralph Caplan, "Design for Travel(ers)," in *Bon Voyage: Designs for Travel*, Deborah Sampson Shinn, J. G. Links, et al. (New York: Cooper-Hewitt Museum, 1986), 95–127, 101.

Chapter 1

1 Tennessee Williams, *A Streetcar Named Desire* (New York: New Directions, 2004), 44.

2 For more on pockets in relationship to gender and class, see Chelsea G. Summers, "The Politics of Pockets,"

Racked, September 19, 2016, https://www.racked.com/2016/9/19/12865560/politics-of-pockets-suffragettes-women.

3 All material on Georgian London from Amanda Vickery, *Behind Closed Doors: At Home in Georgian England* (New Haven and London: Yale University Press, 2009), 26, 38–39.

4 Hans Ulrich Obrist, "Ever Airport: Notes on Taryn Simon's Contraband," *Contraband* (New York: Steidl/Gagosian Gallery, 2010), 7.

5 Ibid.

6 Obrist, "Ever Airport," 9.

7 Simon, quoted by Obrist, "Ever Airport: Notes on Taryn Simon's Contraband," 13.

8 Obrist, "Ever Airport," 15.

9 https://www.icp.org/exhibitions/the-mexican-suitcase-traveling-exhibition

10 David Chazan, "Researchers study 17th century undelivered letters found in a leather trunk," *Telegraph*, November 9, 2005, http://www.telegraph.co.uk/news/worldnews/europe/netherlands/11982846/Researchers-study-17th-century-undelivered-letters-found-in-a-leather-trunk.html.

11 Herman Melville, *Bartleby the Scrivener* (New York: Melville House, 2010), 64.

12 Jane Austen, *Northanger Abbey* (New York: Penguin, 1995), 143.

13 Austen, *Northanger Abbey*.

14 Ibid., 144.

15 Ibid., 148.

16 Ibid.

17 Ibid., 149.

18 Ibid., 150.

19 Ibid.

20 Lily Koppel, *The Red Leather Diary: Reclaiming a Life Through the Pages of a Lost Journal* (New York: Harper Collins, 2008), 1.

21 Koppel, *The Red Leather Diary*, 7.

22 Darby Penney and Peter Stastny, *The Lives They Left Behind: Suitcases from a State Hospital Attic* (New York: Bellevue Literary Press, 2008), Prologue, 25.

23 See Ingrid and Konrad Scheurmann, *For Walter Benjamin: Documentation, Essays and a Sketch*, 3 vols. (Bonn: Inter Nationes, 1993).

24 Ovid, *The Poems of Exile*, trans. Peter Green (Berkeley and Los Angeles: University of California Press, 2005), 19.

25 Ovid, *Poems of Exile*, 10.

26 Ibid., 25.

27 *Virginia Quarterly Review* 93, no. 2 (Spring 2017): 9.

28 Holland Cotter, "For Migrants Headed North, the Things They Carried to the End," *New York Times*, March 3, 2017, https://www.nytimes.com/2017/03/03/arts/design/state-of-exception-estado-de-excepcion-parsons-mexican-immigration.html.

29 Ibid.

30 David Foster Wallace, *A Supposedly Fun Thing I'll Never Do Again: Essays and Arguments* (New York: Back Bay Books, 1997), 270.

31 For more on Brian Goggin's "Samson" installation at the Sacramento Airport, see Christopher Schaberg, *The Textual*

Life of Airports: Reading the Culture of Flight (New York: Continuum International Publishing Group, 2011), Chapter 9.

32 "Titanic luggage turns up 99 years too late," *Yorkshire Post*, November 2, 2013, http://www.yorkshirepost.co.uk/news/titanic-luggage-turns-up-99-years-too-late-1-6208609.

33 "Only one passenger saved his baggage," *New York Times*, April 24, 1912, www.encyclopedia-titanica.org/baggage-saved.html.

Chapter 2

1 William Shakespeare, *Henry V*, ed. T.W. Craik (New York: Bloomsbury Arden, 1995).

2 Tim O'Brien, *The Things They Carried* (New York: Penguin Books, 1990), 3.

3 O'Brien, *The Things They Carried*, 5.

4 Steven Connor, *Paraphernalia: The Curious Lives of Magical Things* (London: Profile, 2011), 16.

5 Natalie Zarrelli, "The Most Precious Cargo for Lighthouses Across America Was a Traveling Library," *Atlas Obscura*, February 18, 2016, http://www.atlasobscura.com/articles/the-most-precious-cargo-for-lighthouses-across-america-was-a-traveling-library.

6 Paula Byrne, *The Real Jane Austen: A Life in Small Things* (New York: HarperCollins, 2013), 267.

7 Byrne, *The Real Jane Austen*, 268.

8 Freydis Jane Welland, "The History of Jane Austen's Writing Desk," *Persuasions: The Jane Austen Journal* 30 (2008): 125–28.

9 William Shakespeare, *Henry IV, Part 1*, ed. David Scott Kastan (New York: Arden Bloomsbury, 2002).

10 Robert Pinsky, trans., *The Inferno of Dante* (New York: Farrar, Straus and Giroux, 1996), 7.

11 C. D. Wright, *ShallCross* (Port Townsend, WA: Copper Canyon Press), 138.

12 Sinead Morrissey, *Parallax and Selected Poems* (Farrar, Straus and Giroux, 2015), 201.

13 Constance Urdang, "The Luggage," http://www.poetryfoundation.org/poem/176469.

14 Stanley Moss, *A History of Color: New and Collected Poems* (New York: Seven Stories Press, 2003), 34.

15 Paul K. Saint-Amour, "Over-Assemblage: Ulysses and the Boite-en-Valise from Above," in *Cultural Studies of James Joyce*, ed. R. Brandon Kershner (Amsterdam and New York: European Joyce Studies 15, 2003), 21–58, 43.

16 Derek Attridge, "Unpacking the Portmanteau, or Who's Afraid of *Finnegans Wake*?" in *On Puns*, ed. Jonathan Culler (Oxford: Basil Blackwell, 1988), 140–55, 145 and 148.

17 *Texas Quarterly* IV (winter, 1961): 50.

18 Lewis Carroll, *Alice's Adventures in Wonderland & Through the Looking-Glass* (New York: Bantam, 1981), 179.

19 Francis Huxley, *The Raven and the Writing Desk* (New York: Harper & Row, 1976), 62.

20 Mary Ruefle, *Trances of the Blast* (Seattle and New York: Wave Books, 2013), 13.

21 Huxley, *The Raven and the Writing Desk*, 121.

22 Katherine Mansfield, *Stories*, ed. Jeffrey Myers, 1920 (New York: Vintage, 1991), 157.

23 Ibid.

24 Sergei Dolatov, *The Suitcase*, tr. Antonina W. Bouis (Berkeley: Counterpoint, 1986), 129.

25 Ernest Hemingway, *A Moveable Feast* (New York: Charles Scribner's Sons, 1964), 74.

26 Orhan Pamuk, "My Father's Suitcase," *New Yorker*, December 26, 2006, http://www.newyorker.com/magazine/2006/12/25/my-fathers-suitcase.

Chapter 3

1 Eric J. Leed, *The Mind of the Traveler: From Gilgamesh to Global Tourism* (New York: Basic Books, 1991), 2.

2 Richard Ford, *Between Them: Remembering My Parents* (New York: Ecco, 2017), 42.

3 Jack Kerouac, *On the Road* (New York: Penguin 1955), 11–12.

4 See Michelle Dean, "Read it and keep: is it time to reassess the 'beach read'?" *Guardian*, June 2, 2016, https://www.theguardian.com/books/2016/jun/02/beach-read-summer-books-holiday-vacation, and Ilana Masad, "When Totally Normal Books About Girls Turned Into 'Beach Reads,'" *Broadly*, June 20, 2017, https://broadly.vice.com/en_us/article/when-totally-normal-books-about-girls-turned-into-beach-reads.

5 "No surprises there then: women DO pack too much when they go on holiday," *Daily Mail*, August 30, 2010, http://www.dailymail.co.uk/news/article-1307365/Women-DO-pack-holiday.html?mrn_rm=als1.

6 Hitha Palepu, *How To Pack* (New York: Clarkson Potter, 2017), 19.

7 Alice Oswald, *Dart* (London: Faber & Faber, 2002), 3.

8 Roland Barthes, *Mythologies*, tr. Annette Lavers (New York: Hill and Wang, 1972), 65–66.

9 Barthes, *Mythologies*, 65.

10 Ibid.

11 Susan Stewart, *On Longing: Narratives of the Miniature, the Gigantic, the Souvenir, the Collection* (Durham: Duke University Press, 1993), 68.

12 P. L. Travers, *Mary Poppins* (New York: Harcourt, 1981), 11.

13 Travers, *Mary Poppins*, 203.

14 Lucy Maud Montgomery, *Anne of Green Gables* (New York: Puffin Books, 2014), 16.

15 Montgomery, *Anne of Green Gables*, 17.

16 Ibid., 18.

Chapter 4

1 "Introduction," *The Gendered Object*, ed. Pat Kirkham (Manchester and New York: Manchester University Press, 1996), 9.

2 *Seinfeld,* "The Reverse Peephole," season 9, episode 12 (1998).

3 Ralph Caplan, "Designs for Travel(ers)," *Designs for Travel* (New York: Cooper-Hewitt Museum, 1986), 95–127, 125.

4 Jane Austen, *Selected Letters*, ed. Vivien Jones (Oxford: Oxford University Press, 2004), 32.

Chapter 5

1 Elaine Scarry, *On Beauty and Being Just* (Princeton: Princeton University Press, 1999), 16.

2 Austen, *Selected Letters*, 29–30.

3 Ibid., 85, 87.

4 Ibid., 166.

5 Joe Yogerst, "Best and Worst Airlines for Lost Luggage," *Travel+ Leisure*, February 13, 2013, http://www.travelandleisure.com/slideshows/best-and-worst-airlines-for-lost-luggage.

6 Scott McCartney, "Baggage Claim: Airlines Are Winning the War on Lost Luggage," *Wall Street Journal*, June 4, 2014, https://www.wsj.com/articles/baggage-claim-airlines-are-winning-the-war-on-lost-luggage-1401922595.

INDEX

Note: Page references for illustrations appear in *italics*.